REVOLUTION
OF LOVE AND BALANCE

3/16

REVOLUTION
OF LOVE AND BALANCE

GEORGE VERWER

STL BOOKS
P.O. Box 48, Bromley, Kent, England
P.O. Box 28, Waynesboro, Georgia 30830, USA

© 1977 George Verwer
Revised edition 1980
First reprint 1981

STL Books are published by Send The Light Trust, 9 London Road,
Bromley, Kent, England

ISBN 0 903843 32 3

Covers printed by Penderel Press Ltd., London

Set, printed and bound by Cox & Wyman Ltd, Reading

Contents

Introduction

The four messages which make up this book were originally given as part of the discipleship training programme of Operation Mobilisation. They are presented in this printed form in the light of the impact their content has had on the lives of thousands of Christian young people who have passed through this international movement over the years. Young people who have longed for deeper reality in their own daily experience of Christ. Young people whose lives have convinced us time and time again of the need to share in every possible way with our fellow believers in Christ the revolutionary nature of His teachings balanced by the experience of His love. We hope that this small book will communicate something of this message that the Holy Spirit has already used so powerfully in our own lives.

Revolution of Love

Galatians 5:22–26 – verses that should be deeply etched in the mind of every Christian:

But the fruit of the Spirit is love, joy, peace, longsuffering, gentleness, goodness, faith [better translated 'faithfulness'], meekness, temperance; against such there is no law. And they that are Christ's have crucified the flesh with the affections and lusts.

If we live in the Spirit, let us also walk in the Spirit. Let us not be desirous of vain glory, provoking one another, envying one another.

*   *   *

The fruit of the Spirit is love. We believe Christianity is a 'revolution of love', and we are convinced that there is nothing more important in all the world than this.

Now let us clarify our concept of love. In 1 John we are told that 'God is love'. This is a clear and simply-stated definition: God is love.

In other words, true love is from God . . . it does not exist apart from Him. We know that God is One. Therefore, we cannot think of God the Father without thinking of love; we cannot think of the Lord Jesus Christ without thinking of love; we cannot think of the Holy Spirit without thinking of love. There is no separation. God does not send love. He does not manufacture it. God *is* love.

Now that appears to be a very simple statement, but I am convinced that only an extremely small percentage of believers have really come to grips with this truth. A seminary student said to me, 'I finally listened to all your tapes and all your messages, and it has only just dawned on me what you mean by "revolution of love" – what you mean when you say, "God is Love".'

As we see the state of the church world-wide and the state of the average believer, it is easy to become discouraged. We look for discipleship; we look for those who are labouring together in unity, in prayer, in power . . . and we see quarrels and divisions, complacency and mediocrity.

Many young people are asking, 'Why is the church in such a state? . . . Why is Christianity today making so little impact?'

Many talk about the 'secret'. Somehow we have missed the secret, they feel, and therefore the church is as it is. They think that perhaps what is needed is a new book that will reveal this secret and bring deliverance and restoration to the church.

Now it seems to me that it would not be very fair of God to keep secret the most basic ingredient of Christian effectiveness. And I do not believe it is a secret.

The Basic Message

There is, I believe, a basic ingredient which is largely lacking in Christianity today, and the lack of it is the source of most of our problems. It is the cancer which is eating away at the church, but it is no secret. In fact, it is so non-secretive that it is written on almost every page of the New Testament. And yet, because the heart of man is deceitful and desperately wicked, and because we are so bent on our own way, we do not see (or seeing we do not believe) that the basic message of the New Testament is *love*!

It is my absolute conviction that most of us miss this most obvious and most repeated message, even while laying great emphasis on 'sound doctrine'.

Well, I would like to ask you, 'What is sound doctrine?' We have long discussions on the Second Coming, on the Atoning Work of Christ, on the Church, the Holy Spirit, etc., etc. But what about love and humility and brokenness? These usually go into a separate category, but I want to tell you that if your doctrine does not include love and humility and brokenness, then your doctrine is not sound.

There are thousands, even millions, of people who claim to be 'orthodox Christians' because they cling to a certain set of beliefs in accord with the Bible. They are aware that they do not practise much humility, but they do not think that makes them any less orthodox. They are aware that they do not really love the brethren in Christ (especially those who are different from them), but that does not cause them to think their doctrine is not sound.

They admit that they know nothing of 'laying down their lives' for the brethren and esteeming the other as better than themselves, and yet they consider themselves fundamental, orthodox Christians.

Oh, what an error this is! This false concept – thinking we can be orthodox without having humility, thinking we can be sound in doctrine without having love, thinking we can be fundamental evangelicals though our lives do not show forth the fruit of the

Spirit – this is the greatest error that has hit Christianity even before or since the Reformation!

Doctrine cannot be separated from practical living. Brethren, I do not see Jesus Christ as a dual personality, partly doctrine and partly moral, trying to bring two separate realms of truth into our minds. He was not on the one hand trying to teach us what we call doctrine, and on the other hand trying to make us morally right. It is completely wrong to think of doctrine as being apart from living.

'Oh,' someone says, 'there is a good, evangelical Christian . . . he has good sound doctrine. He does not have much love for others and he is not very humble, but he's very sound in doctrine.' He is *not* sound in doctrine if he does not love the brethren. What do we read in 1 John 4:8? 'He that loveth not knoweth not God.'

There is no sounder doctrine than love, and apart from love there is no sound doctrine. This is the basis of all Bible doctrine. You take the base out and everything you build will eventually collapse.

The Wise Man

Let's look in James, chapter 3, at some verses that have deeply spoken to my heart. Verse 13: 'Who is a wise man and endued with knowledge among you?'

Well, who is he? Who is wise and endued with knowledge? Is he the one who knows all the answers? Is he the one who has the solution to every problem . . . the one who always knows which road to take, how to witness and lead souls to Christ, how to distribute literature? Is this the wise man in your midst? Possibly. But not necessarily.

The Bible says, 'Who is the wise man ... among you? Let him show out of a good conversation [or life] his works with meekness of wisdom.'

In other words, God says to the man who has the correct theory and who knows what the Bible teaches, 'All right, let's see it in your life. First, above everything else, let's see it lived out. If a man is truly wise, then he is truly meek.'

Reading on in James, we find that certain factors disqualify a person from this wisdom. 'But if you have bitter envying and strife in your hearts, glory not, and lie not against the truth.' When we claim to be sound in doctrine and to have New Testament truth, and yet our lives are not filled with meekness, but rather with bitterness, we are actually lying against the truth with our lives. This is the great problem everywhere, today.

Look at the next verse: 'This wisdom descendeth not from above, but is earthly, sensual, devilish.' Do you see what that means?

An Illustration

Let me illustrate this kind of earthly 'wisdom' with an incident that occurred recently. A brother made a mistake in the practical realm. One of his co-workers, who never did capture this revolution of love, knew that the other was in the wrong.

Very quickly he said, 'This is wrong. You should not have done it.' The other brother, in a bit of excitement said, 'Well, I was told to do it this way.' The first, a little more excitedly, said, 'Well, I know it is not right. This is what you should have done.' And soon they had a full-scale argument.

Later on, I talked to the one who claimed to be right.

I said to him, 'Do you feel you were right in that situation?'

'Absolutely,' he said. 'I was right and everybody around here knows I was right!' And he had managed to convince everyone else that he was right.

Then I said, 'Tell me, when you spoke to him, were you in the flesh or in the Spirit?'

He stopped at that and thought for a minute. 'Well, I don't suppose that I was really what you would call in the Spirit.'

I said, 'Well then, you were in the flesh.' He was a bit hesitant but said, 'All right, I admit that I was in the flesh, but I was right.'

I said, 'But dear brother, doesn't the Word of God say that from the flesh cometh no good thing?'

He wasn't right! The way I think, the way I believe Christ thought, the way I believe the New Testament teaches, he was absolutely wrong because truth never comes without moral quality and you cannot tell the truth without love.

The curse of today is orthodoxy without love, orthodoxy without power, orthodoxy without the life of our Lord Jesus Christ.

When we move into the Catholic world or the Muslim world or the Communist world, remember that no matter how right we are about an issue, the minute we act without love, we are in the flesh and not abiding in Christ, and it is sin. No matter how much 'truth' comes from your mouth, it is not truth.

That is what the Bible says here. This 'wisdom' that does not come with meekness and gentleness and love is not wisdom. It is sensual, devilish. Some of the most horrible and unbelievable situations arise in the ranks of Christianity amongst those who have 'lip truth' but do not live the truth. And what a stench it is to God!

The next verse says, 'For where envying and strife is, there is confusion and every evil work.' How we have seen this in our work. The moment that envy creeps in the picture, no matter how much 'orthodoxy' there is, or how much truth is floating around, the result will be just what is described here – confusion. And every evil work follows close behind.

Pure and Peaceable

Then verse seventeen: 'But the wisdom that is from above is first pure'. Do you see it? The wisdom that comes from above is first, not orthodox, but pure. And whenever what we say, and do, is not of the highest moral quality, then it is not from above, but is the earthly, sensual, devilish pseudo-wisdom of the world.

God's wisdom is first always pure, then it is peaceable. Alan Redpath says when you know that you are not in the Spirit, you know you are a little upset, then never open your mouth! I like the way he puts it: 'At that moment, literally force yourself back into the will of God.' Force yourself back into the will of God, and then speak. But never open your mouth when you are not in the Spirit, for no matter how hard you try you will never speak with true wisdom.

How many times have you hurt someone because you spoke too soon? Husbands, how many times have you hurt your wife because you did not keep quiet a few minutes longer? I know how many times I could have kicked myself all over our little room because I did not wait a little longer before I spoke.

The Bible says, 'The wisdom that comes from above

is first pure, then peaceable, then gentle.' Gentle! What do you know about that, young zealot? You know it is easy to be zealous between the ages of 17 and 35. That's right. It isn't hard for energetic youth to be zealous. 'Ho, I am out to conquer the world. Everybody is going to hear about Jesus Christ!' And away we go in the zeal of the flesh until around the age of 30 or 35, or after the first child comes, and then we suddenly discover that our 'zeal thermometer' is beginning to drop. Finally, we have to admit that we have been working in the energy of the flesh. Youthful lusts! Youthful lusts directed into Christian activity. Youthful zeal! Youthful enthusiasm! But youthful gentleness? – *the wisdom that is from above is gentle*.

How Do You Respond?

And it is 'easy to be intreated'. What does that mean . . . easy to be intreated? Some of us love to read the Bible just for the sake of Bible reading, and we go over these verses time and time again and haven't a clue what they really mean. 'Easy to be intreated' means easy to be taught and corrected. This quality is tested when, for instance, you are washing dishes, and someone says: 'Look, why don't you use this dish towel . . . and, oh my, you need to put some soap in the water.' Are you easy to be intreated in such a circumstance? Or, perhaps, you are loading a vehicle with books and a brother says, 'Don't put them in that way. Do it like this.' How do you respond? The way you respond to correction is a great test of what Jesus is doing in your life. When someone comes up and puts his arm around your shoulder and says, 'Sorry, brother, but you are doing it all wrong,' what is your reaction? 'Praise the

Lord. I appreciate that brother.' Is that your reaction?

One of the greatest tests in the Christian life comes when you are confronted with correction and criticism.

Anyone can live for Christ when he is receiving pats on the back. Anyone! I mean outwardly. As long as you are doing your job well and are being appreciated, you can lean on that psychological 'crutch'. But when you are criticised, rightly or wrongly, then you can lean only on Jesus.

This is exactly what we need to do, and possibly that is why God sometimes allows the props to be knocked from under us, and puts us under fire in the form of criticism. We need to learn to work only for His 'Well done, thou good and faithful servant.'

Let's look on to some other tests of true wisdom. Next, it says, the wisdom that cometh from above is full of mercy and good fruit, without partiality and without hypocrisy. Full of mercy – towards the weaker brother, towards the offending brother, towards the guilty brother; full of mercy and full of good fruit. It is without partiality and without hypocrisy.

This is orthodox doctrine. And I pray that if anyone can show me that this is wrong thinking or that I am misinterpreting the New Testament, and that it is possible for me to have sound doctrine without peace, purity, gentleness, etc., that he will show me. But please do not try to tell me some dear brother has a miserable life but sound doctrine, because I just will not believe you. Sound doctrine and wisdom that comes from above always comes with a Bible-linked life. This conviction is the core of all true Christian work.

The greatest desire of our hearts for the church and

for every believer is to see this linking of sound doctrine and sound life together.

Explosive Message

Now let us turn to 1 John 3. I want to tell you that as I have gone through this First Epistle of John it has rocked me! This epistle is so loaded with revolution and dynamite that if we had reached the average Communist with this message before the message of Marx reached him, we would have many more born-again Russians.

I will never forget that young, red-hot Communist who came into our office in Lancashire, England. We took him into this epistle and showed him the teachings of Jesus, and two weeks later he got down on his knees in the kitchen and gave his life to Christ. I tell you, this message of First John is right from the heart of God for this generation!

Now let's see what God says to us through 1 John 3:11. 'This is the message that ye heard from the beginning, that we should love one another.'

What is our message as Christians? Sometimes it seems that our primary message is 'believe'. Believe on the Lord Jesus Christ and thou shalt be saved. Believe on the Lord Jesus Christ and afterwards everything will be fine. Well, perhaps you find it so. But when I read 'believe' in the New Testament, I find something that is like an atomic bomb. When a man really believes on Jesus Christ, it is revolution becoming operative, a revolution of love. You cannot separate the one from the other.

People are always having trouble over this question of repentance . . . what does it mean when it says 'repent and believe'? Are we saved through only believing or believing plus a few good works? It is through believing only. But real belief brings revolution. It results in moral action. There is no such thing as real belief without repentance. 'Believe on the Lord Jesus Christ and thou shalt be saved.' Good works will never save you, no matter how hard (or long) you work, or how many works you do. But when you have believed, you are going to work as a result, because the Holy Spirit is the Author of good works.

Wanting 'Experiences'

A few years ago, a dear emotional Christian woman told me about people who were having experiences in the Spirit. I asked, 'When the Holy Spirit works in such a mighty way, shouldn't that produce a moral revolution? Shouldn't the man who has had such experiences afterwards be filled with love and joy and peace? Shouldn't he forsake all that he has, as we are told the early Christians did in the book of Acts? Shouldn't he lay down his life for others?'

The lady said to me, 'Sometimes the Holy Spirit comes just to give us joy and a wonderful experience and blessing.' I said to her, 'You mean that sometimes the Holy Spirit comes apart from His holiness?' She began to ponder that.

I tell you, the Holy Spirit does not come apart from His holiness. The emphasis is not on Spirit but on Holy, and He cannot come without His moral character. It is for this reason that we measure a person's experience with the Spirit (although we prefer to say the Spirit's experience with the person), on the basis of his moral quality.

You cannot separate the word 'believe' in its Biblical context from the word 'love'. Do not try! How many men we have in our churches, leaders some of them, who speak to a congregation from the Word of God, but in their homes know nothing more about loving their wives than the man in the next house who cannot stand his! And they go on and on, continuing to think they are spiritual men with just a besetting sin of not being able to really love their wives. Oh, how absolutely heart-breaking! Do you not see the absolute incompatibility of such views? So many Christians cannot get along with their neighbours! Oh, how sad . . .!

If your 'besetting sin' is that you cannot love people, you are in great danger. We do not mean to say that it will always be easy to love people, or that you will not have battles about it. It will be a daily fist fight with the forces of darkness, but the Word of God clearly teaches that we are to love one another.

We cannot have fellowship with God without having fellowship with our brethren in Christ. We cannot love God without first loving the brethren.

Look at chapter four, verse 20:

'If a man say, I love God, and hateth his brother, he is a liar: for he that loveth not his brother whom he hath seen, how can he love God whom he hath not seen?'

The prevalent idea today is that if we love God enough we will eventually love our brethren. But when I read this verse, I hit the floor because it says very clearly, 'He that loveth not his brother whom he hath seen, how can he love God whom he hath not seen?' If there is any brother or any sister who you do not love, actively, operationally, then something is wrong.

I am of the conviction that 99 per cent of the prayers

of Christians do not get any higher than the ceiling because of lack of love. If the prayers of the saints were being answered during these days, the world would have been evangelised long ago. At the prayer meetings we attend, there is always tremendous verbal exercise. Fantastic things are asked of God. 'Lord, we claim this country for you.' 'We believe, Father, that you will open a way into China.' 'Lord, we trust you to bring 100 new people to the meeting tonight.' And on and on we go, and yet all the time there is another brother in the same prayer meeting whom we cannot stand. Oh, not that we don't love him . . . we would just rather not be around him. Of course, we don't hate him . . . it is just that our personalities conflict!

Love Your Enemies

There are hundreds and hundreds of watered-down phrases for not loving other people. 'Oh, I love him in the Lord, but I don't like his mannerisms . . . Susie is all right, but she is so hard to get to know . . . This one has emotional problems and that one comes from a low social background.'

In the sight of God it is all hypocrisy. God never said in His Word, 'Love your brother if he is a keen chap, well-dressed, zealous, a soul-winner . . . and if he loves you.' No! on the other hand, Christ told us in the Sermon on the Mount that real love does not begin until we love our enemies!

This whole concept of loving our enemies is, for the average person of today, nothing but an outdated theological phrase, so impossible for the human nature to attain that it is never taken seriously, even among Christians.

We know nothing of it, nothing of really loving a man who cannot tolerate us, who speaks evil of us, spites us, does not like us, or the way we operate. More often we cannot love even the people around us with whom we live and work.

Some time ago, someone told me flatly that he loved everybody. I replied: 'You are saying quite a bit, brother, when you say that.' But he was insistent that he loved everybody. I happened to know of at least one person to whom he didn't bother to say 'hello' in the morning. He could pass this person several times a day, never showing kindness – not a smile. I asked, 'Do you really love him?' He said, 'Of course I do. Well, I mean I love all the believers.'

Do you see? It is all here in the head. There is no love without action! Potentially he may have loved him. Theoretically he may have loved him. But it was not a reality.

God's Work, Not Ours

A Christian is at all times indwelt by the Holy Spirit of God and so has all His potential for this tremendous revolution of love. The Holy Spirit is there, just waiting to take possession of a man and make him loving. He is just waiting to move that man to volunteer for the washing-up, for cleaning the toilets, for cleaning out the back of the trucks. The Holy Spirit is waiting to make him ready to take the low road and jump ahead of his brother in the dirty tasks. But what happens? Our pride, stubbornness, and egocentric living, quench the action of the Holy Spirit in our lives.

Jesus Christ said, 'Love thy neighbour as thyself!' Oh, isn't that amazing! I am so glad that Jesus was more intelligent than Aristotle or Socrates. Isn't it nice that we Christians have the truth? But what has been the result in the practical realm? What has it been in India, for instance? Certain missionaries went with their heads in the clouds, shut themselves away from the people in their missionary compounds, put locks on all the doors, and taught, 'Love thy neighbour as thyself.' And in Africa, what have been the results? Well, in many places, the missionaries are saying, 'We love our neighbours as ourselves. But, well, the coloured people had better use the back doors, and clean the houses, and be the nannies for the little white children.'

What, then, does all this talk about love really mean? 'Love your neighbour as yourself.' Well, how do you love yourself? How did you love yourself this morning? You got out of bed groggily, wiped all the sleep out of your eyes, went to the mirror and said, 'Oh, how I love you! You are so wonderful; I love you, I love you, I love you so much!' Did you? Well, if you do that too many mornings someone might call in a psychiatrist for you. That is not the way we love ourselves! That is the way we love our neighbours. That's right! 'The Lord bless you dear brother. Yes, yes, the Lord bless you. The Lord do wonderful things for you.'

We sign our letters 'love in Christ', and think, 'Well, that's another one out of the way.' But that is not the way we love ourselves. Perhaps we can understand love better if we use the word 'care'. You have been caring for yourself all day long, ever since this morning when you woke up and your self-love automatically went right into action. You had a wash and shave, brushed your teeth, used a few creams and lotions, and put the proper amount of clothes on to keep your body warm. Shortly after getting out of bed, you had a little pain in your tummy – very slight, but enough to get you into action. Immediately you started toward the coffeepot and bread and jam.

If you are really honest you will probably have to say that as you came to the table you were not wondering if there was enough kitchen help, if there were some in the group unable to come to breakfast this morning, people to whom you could take some food. No. You sat down, and noticing that there was no margarine on your table, you began to look for some on another table. You were taking care of yourself automatically.

I am not saying that this is wrong. Neither does Jesus. It is wonderful that Jesus knows all about us. If humanity could only grasp this truth, we could burn all the psychology books in a good-sized trash can. One leading psychologist recently said that if we took all the straw from the psychology books of our day what we would have left would be far inferior to the Sermon on the Mount.

Oh, for men and women that would follow the revolutionary psychology of the Man who understood the human mind better than Freud, Adler, Jung and all the rest put together.

God doesn't say that you should not love yourself. But He does say that you should love your neighbour in the same way as you love yourself. He does not say that you should not have breakfast, but He does say you should be concerned about your brother's breakfast as well. Oh, I tell you this thrills me. I do not know if I am communicating . . . I can only say what Brother Bakht Singh often says when he is preaching: 'Well, that is as much as you can get from a clay pot.'

And I know that I do not express myself well many times, but I just pray that the Spirit of God will show you what this revolution of love really is – what it means to obey the second commandment of Jesus Christ daily from the time you get up in the morning until you go to bed at night. Only this will make an impact on such a materialistic age as this one. Our tracts will not do it. Our Bibles will not do it. Jesus said, 'By this shall all men know that you are my disciples, if you have love one to another.' Not if you have sound doctrine and zeal. No! They will know it if you love the brethren. This is the greatest challenge in the Word of God – to love men as Christ loved them, to love them as we love ourselves, to care for men as we care for ourselves.

Forsaking All

The only logical outcome of such love is forsaking all! I believe that when a man falls in love with Jesus, it can be compared in some ways to a young man falling in love with a girl he has dreamed about all his life. The day they are married, he transfers his bank account and puts it in her name, he takes out an insurance policy in the name of his beloved. In other words, because he loves her, he gives her all he has.

Some of you are having trouble with this message of discipleship. Some of you are having trouble with this thing of forsaking all that you have. You are holding back, you know that you are holding back, and you have a conflict within you. You have this conflict and find it so difficult to give up your possessions, and the reason is that your relationship with Jesus Christ is not right. You need to fall in love with Him, and then your greatest joy will be to lay everything you have at His feet. It will not be painful, it will not be as though something were being wrenched from you – it will be joy.

The man who does not know the joy of giving has not yet begun to live, for it is, indeed, more blessed to give than to receive. It is a revolutionary principle of life that our greatest joys come from giving. It is completely contrary to our flesh. By nature we grasp everything to ourselves and we become the centre. But when we become Christ-centred, it is just like centrifugal force, like a whirlwind throwing everything outward and leaving Christ pre-eminent, our one love!

'Love thy neighbour as thyself,' said Jesus. And on another occasion He illustrated in the parable of the Good Samaritan who he meant by neighbour and what He meant by love. Care for your neighbour as you care for yourself. That is why I find it hard to eat breakfast without praying for India, why I find it hard to take a piece of bread and a sip of tea without a pain in my heart for those souls who have no food.

We who claim to have the truth, we evangelicals, we Bible-believers, have become hardened to the need of mankind. The Oxford Group or Moral Rearmament has been known to have more compassion on university campuses in Britain than any evangelical group. Because they were given a shilling a mile to buy food for the starving multitudes, these fellows marched in a great line from London to Bristol. That's right! I tell you we are a sham. If I said to you, 'Brother, I would like you to go and distribute tracts tonight and I will give you 5p a tract,' how many tracts would you give out? If I said I would give you £50 cash for every soul you bring to the feet of Jesus Christ, do you think you might study about soul-winning a little more? But tell me, who can put a value on a soul?

We need to see where we are before God. Look at 1 John 3:14. 'We know that we have passed from death unto life, because we love the brethren. He that loveth not his brother abideth in death.'

That is quite blunt, isn't it? You say, 'Oh, I am not abiding in death. I am born again.' How do you know you are born again? Well, there are a number of ways, but one of them is *love*. You raised your hand in a gospel meeting. You said, 'Jesus, I believe in you'. But if you did not go out from that meeting with the seed of the revolution of love in your heart beginning to produce love for the brethren, you were only engaged in a cheap exercise of arms. You were never born again!

The church is filled – and I say this with a pang in my heart – the church is *filled* with unregenerate but 'orthodox' men who have made so-called decisions and claimed to believe in Christ, but whose lives are filled with hatred and bitterness toward their brothers in Christ. It is a delusion – the largest, most detestable sugar-coated pill the devil ever gave out! There is no conversion without revolution. There is no conversion that does not produce the seed of a loving life, tiny though it be in the beginning, and I believe that this is the message God has given us to declare to the world.

Look at the 16th verse: 'Hereby perceive we the love of God, because He laid down His life for us: and we ought to lay down our lives for the brethren.' This is how we know God loves us. This is how we know the love of God, the way we perceive it, the way we understand it. He laid down His life for us. He died for us, He did something. He did not sit up in glory and sing, 'Oh earthlings, I love you, I know you are mine.' He did not do that. That is what we do. We sit in our meetings and sing, 'My Jesus, I love thee,' and yet many times we are not on speaking terms with the man in the pew beside us. Any man who can sing that without going out from that meeting to show love in his life has passed through a religious pantomime which is an insult to Almighty God. Absolutely! And I am convinced that the world will never be evangelised except we experience the love of God in our hearts towards others!

We are not going to go into all the technical terms. We will not list the points – one, two, three – how you can experience the love of God. It is quite clear that there are no spiritual pep pills. But what I am trying to do is create hunger. Hunger in your heart to be like Jesus! Hunger in your heart to know this life-changing love! Hunger that will get you so absolutely starved for God that eventually, through knowing Him, His love will be spread abroad in your life!

'Blessed is the man who hungers and thirsts after righteousness, for he shall be filled.'

The first step in this revolution is to want it! It is a universal law that when you want something badly, whether it is good or bad, if you continue to crave that desire it will take hold of your subconscious mind and eventually you will get it. How many times has it happened that someone has asked you the name of a person and you said, 'I have his name right on the tip of my tongue . . . now what is it?' You were motivated to want to know that name. You tried again, 'What is that man's name?' And again, 'Now what is his name?' And then you laid it aside for a while. You thought you had laid it aside. But you had fed a desire into your inner being, into your subconscious mind a question, a desire, and the wheels started going. Ten minutes later, completely without conscious effort, what came into your mind? The name of your friend!

Think for a minute of Charles Whitman, that young university student in Texas who went up into the tower on the campus and began to shoot people at random. This thought had come into his mind many times before. He had even mentioned it to his psychiatrist. But I am sure that the first time it occurred to him he was shocked and thought, 'I could never do anything like that.' Nevertheless, the thought continued to come to him more and more frequently. It was suppressed and suppressed into his subconscious mind until finally it took possession of him totally and he was powerless against his craving.

This is what happens when you lust. Every time you want something that is not of God, you sow a thought. And soon it will result in action and you will reap the harvest of sin in your life. Remember the verse, 'And I gave them their request, and I sent leanness to their soul!' Be careful what you want!

Maybe you have a desire you wouldn't express to me . . . or your best friend . . . or even to your husband or wife. Maybe it is new clothes, maybe it is marriage, maybe it is recognition. Perhaps it is something legitimate, if God were to give it to you. But the desire is so strong in you and you think, 'Others have it', and the seed of envy is sown in your heart. And then you think, 'Why can't I have it?' and the seed of bitterness is sown. And that desire is persistent and you begin to think you can't live without this thing and soon, God will let you have it. But be careful, because you will also get leanness unto your soul.

Brokenness

In the same way I am convinced that if you want a life of love, if you want to be conformed to the image of Jesus Christ, if you want to join that remnant of people who are fed up with words, hymns, and hypocrisy, if you want reality and revolution in your life, then you will have it. If you are starved for such a life, you will have it. 'Blessed is the man who hungers and thirsts after righteousness, for he shall be filled.'

It will take time. Perhaps you have heard this before and you say, 'Last year I heard a message like this and I got on my knees and wept before God. I said, "Lord, I want to be loving, I want to be humble, I want to be gentle, I want to be a servant." ' And now you look back at the past year, and it is not very impressing. Do not be discouraged. What God wants of us is *brokenness*. He wants us to realise that in our flesh there is no good thing, that we cannot love the brethren, that from the time we get up in the morning until we go to bed at night we live a life of utter selfishness, except when God interrupts us. Do you want this? Do you want to know something of loving your enemies? Do you want to know something of being a servant, something of being easily entreated, of weeping for men who are without food and without Christ?

I will never forget a one-day campaign we had in Bombay, when the Lord laid it on our hearts to distribute a half million tracts in one day. After having distributed some 400,000 tracts throughout the day, we had a meeting in the evening. As we closed that meeting we said that if anyone was constrained to go back into the streets with tracts, we still had a few left . . . about 100,000! There were several volunteers. I had absolutely no desire to go out that night with more tracts. It was 11 p.m., we had started the day at 5 a.m., and I had worked through the night before on the maps of the city. I was tired. I did not feel any love tingling through me. And as I started out, I just stopped where I was and turned my eyes upon Jesus. I saw Him going the second mile – I saw Him going up Calvary's hill for me. That was love! It was not cheap sentiment. It was not a letter signed, 'I love you'. It was action. And I said to myself that if Jesus could go the extra mile for me, then surely, He could help me go the extra mile for those others whom He loved. Love is action . . . 'If you love me, keep my commandments.'

We went out into the streets of Bombay again, and around midnight I could see for about a quarter of a mile in front of us around five thousand men and women sleeping on the pavement. I've never before seen such a sight in my life. I had two big bags filled with tracts and for the first time in my life, I went from 'bed to bed', giving out tracts!

This world in which we live is a sick world. It is a world of misery and tragedy such as most of us cannot begin to imagine. Millions are sleeping on pavements, starving to death, knowing nothing of the love of God for them. The church sings, 'My Jesus, I love Thee'. And at the same time 150,000 people a day slip away into eternity. And we say that we love them. I say we don't. If we loved them with Christ's love, we wouldn't stop until we had sold a million books and distributed 100 million tracts. And as we did it, our tears would bathe these lost souls. I know too little about it. I have wept little over souls and much over my unloving heart. But I can say tonight before God, '*I want it!*' You can take all that I have! You can take my family (and I do not say this lightly), *but I want a life of love! I want God!*

If you can say this, we believe you will have a blessed time! But if your primary desire is Christian service, Christian activity, Christian fellowship, no matter how good that thing might be, I do not believe you will be happy.

Heartfelt Prayer

Let us pray . . .

In silent prayer before the Lord, if you really mean it, I want you to cry to Him to teach you to love, to break you of self, pride, stubbornness, that the love of Christ, shed abroad in your heart through the Holy Spirit, might be operative daily, hourly, moment by moment.

Cry to Him to teach you to love your enemy, to love your critic, not in word, but in deed. Cry to Him that you want love, you want Jesus, you want God, for God is love!

Pseudo-Discipleship

We have heard much about what a disciple is, but in this message I want to speak about what a disciple is not!

There are many in our day who pretend to be disciples. Always within our own ranks there are those who either pretend to be disciples, or who are deceived into thinking they are disciples. Could it be that even in the ranks of a group where the workers receive no salaries and preach Christ supposedly because they love Him, there could be pseudo-disciples?

Yes, without a doubt it is possible, and I am convinced that it is God's desire to purge every true work of His of false disciples.

Let's read Acts 5:1–11:

> But there was a man named Ananias (with his wife Sapphira) who sold some property, and brought only part of the money, claiming it was the full price. (Sapphira had agreed to this deception.) But Peter said, 'Ananias, Satan has filled your heart. When you claimed this was the full price, you were lying to the Holy Spirit. The property was yours to sell or not, as you wished. And after selling it, it was yours to decide how much to give. How could you do a thing like this? You weren't lying to us, but to God.'
>
> As soon as Ananias heard these words, he fell to the

floor, dead! Everyone was terrified, and the younger
men covered him with a sheet and took him out and
buried him.

About three hours later his wife came in, not
knowing what had happened. Peter asked her, 'Did
you people sell your land for such and such a price?'
'Yes,' she replied, 'we did.' And Peter said, 'How
could you and your husband even think of doing a
thing like this – conspiring together to test the Spirit
of God's ability to know what is going on? Just
outside that door are the young men who buried your
husband, and they will carry you out too.'

Instantly she fell to the floor, dead, and the young
men came in and, seeing that she was dead, carried
her out and buried her beside her husband. Terror
gripped the entire church and all others who heard
what had happened. (Living Bible)

Notice that Ananias and Sapphira were not obliged
to give their land. There were no rules about giving all.
There were no pressures put on the believers to sell all.
Their sin was not that they did not give all, but rather
that they were pretending to be what they knew they
were not, pretending in order to receive the praise and
recognition of men. God took them as an example for
His church in all ages, including the twentieth century. If God worked that way today, our churches and
possibly this very hall tonight would be full of corpses!

What impresses me in verse eleven is that, as a result
of God's action, great fear came upon the church. I
have observed that in our day the fear of God is very
rare. In this perverse generation, the majority dare to
presume that God would never punish for sin in this
age of grace. We have had young people in our
summer crusades living blatantly hypocritical lives.
We have had a few young people with us for an entire

year whose lives we discovered were nothing but sham. They lied to their leaders, they lied to me, they lied to their own parents and churches. Thank God, there have been very few such cases. But those few have convinced me that attending conferences, listening to the messages of men of God, participating in a programme of evangelism, etc., is no guarantee against the subtle snares of pseudo-discipleship.

How anyone could attend a conference like some of ours have been and not understand the way of repentance and brokenness is beyond me. But it can happen. 'The heart is deceitful above all things, and desperately wicked: who can know it?' (Jeremiah 17:9).

And so I want to ask that all of us be willing to let the spotlight of God come upon each one of us individually. Please forget, if you will, the other person. It is not for you to shine the spotlight upon your wife or your husband, your friend or your leader. I pray that we will each let the spotlight shine directly on our own life, and with all my heart I want to let it shine full force on me.

The pseudo-disciple pretends to be a learner, but he is not. He has all the outward signs, and many are fooled by him. But he is a fake, a counterfeit. He takes part in all the meetings, he sings, he prays, he evangelises, he sells books, he reads his Bible. But basically his life is not compatible with the principles of discipleship which Christ laid down.

Mr Liar

I have listed twenty-one pseudo-disciples. We will not be able to touch on all of them, but let's consider some of them, beginning with Mr Liar. We might just as well begin here, taking our example straight from Scripture; Ananias and Sapphira were liars. We see from their example that it is possible to be living nominally as a Christian, appearing to follow Christ, taking an active part in the Christian community, and yet be a liar. There have been a few among us who, after some time, confessed to lying on their questionnaire, perhaps about age, perhaps about something in their past which they were afraid would leak out. 'How is that possible among Christians?' you ask. But really, the longer you live among Christians the more you will realise that it is possible! The heart is deceitful and desperately wicked!

Let's be realistic. I wonder if anyone here is in that category tonight? Living a lie! Telling lies, convenient lies, white lies . . . they are the same thing, no matter what the situation. The Bible says, 'all liars will have their part' . . . where? . . . 'in the lake of fire!' I tell you, lying is a dangerous business, and eventually . . . eventually . . . the truth will find you out!

Mr Deceiver

Older and wiser brother to Mr Liar is Mr Deceiver. He is a specialist! He doesn't engage in those straight-forward, crusty lies. He likes the 'around-the-corner' variety. He is a master of giving false impressions. He is often guilty of exaggeration. Perhaps all his life he has craved love and attention, and he finds that when he exaggerates, people listen to him. No one seems very interested in the plain old truth ('I gave out a hundred tracts'); but oh, how people flock around him when he puts a little glow on the story ('I gave out a thousand tracts, and wow! in only one hour!')

Of course, we are all guilty of this from time to time, because we have a sinful nature. But there is a difference between those who are blatantly guilty before God, knowingly practising sin, and those who fall into it unawares in an unguarded moment. I would not classify these latter with Mr Deceiver, but whether it is habitual, or whether it is sudden and unpremeditated, exaggeration is sin of which we must repent. It is so easy for subtle deceit to enter the picture. You are in your room praying, and you have fallen asleep on your knees. Someone enters the room and you wake up suddenly and say, 'Amen,' as if you were deep in prayer. Ever done that? Or you are sitting at your desk munching a nice chocolate bar. There comes a knock on the door, and whoosh, into the drawer goes the chocolate bar! Some think that these little ways of deceiving are sharp and shrewd. God says that they are sin. He tells us that we are to walk honestly before men. In Psalm 51 we find that He 'desireth truth in the inward parts'. Oh, that God will drive that home to our hearts!

Mr Fault-Finder

Another pseudo-disciple who is never far away is Mr Fault-Finder. Just as soon as he makes his appearance, you can be sure he will give you a good headache, because he sees everything that is wrong ... well, all except what is wrong with himself!

He feels that he is a real follower of Christ and that he is really doing a great job for Him. But when he looks around at the others (and he is *always* looking around at the others) all he finds is immaturity, lack of experience, lack of leadership ability, emotional problems ... and so he goes on. He thinks he is following Jesus, but does not realise that his very attitude disqualifies him from following closely after the Lord.

Mr Judge-Others

Mr Fault-Finder is sometimes called by his other name, Mr Judge-Others. He fixes on some little detail, and immediately he puts two and two together and four and four together, but the trouble is that when he adds it all up he gets the wrong answer. There is such a danger in Christian work of judging others – other groups, other individuals. And God hates that! This pseudo-disciple is convinced that he is following Jesus, but he is off on a wide tangent that leads to a deep ditch.

Mr Runaway

An enthusiastic pseudo-disciple who sometimes makes his way into Christian work is Mr Runaway. He bursts in with great zeal, shouting, 'I've been called to China!' and everyone stands back amazed.

Well, we discover a bit later that he has not been called to China, or to any other country. He has only felt a 'call' to run away from something – a home situation, a job failure, a girl who dropped him, or some other unpleasant situation that he does not want to face. Christian service seems like a wonderful escape. Here is a great opportunity, an open door, inviting him to escape from his frustrations and fears and difficult circumstances.

Mr Runaway is not a disciple. And if he feels that he

must run away from the unpleasant, he will be running all his life. It may be that God will want him to return to that very situation and see victory in it, or it *could* be that God will want him to repent of his false motivation and press on from here with true motivation.

I can see how God worked this way in my life. I came to Jesus with false motives. When I was born again in 1955, I didn't go down the aisle of Madison Square Gardens because I loved God. I didn't go because I wanted to be a worshipper of Him and give Him all I had. Not at all! I went down the aisle because I was broken and burdened by my sin and I wanted deliverance and forgiveness. That is pretty selfish, isn't it? Most of us, in fact, came to Christ for selfish reasons – how else could He draw the unregenerate man to Himself? Before he knows Christ he has no pure motives, but once he becomes a Christian, God can modify them. If there is some circumstance in your life you want to run away from, God can use it to draw you to Himself.

It is important, however, that you do not allow false motivation to continue. You may have come to Christ for the wrong reasons, but you should never try to serve Him for the wrong reasons. Running away never solved any problem; running to God always provides an answer.

Mr Girl-Hunter and Miss Husband-Hunter

There is another pseudo-disciple who is seen very frequently within our ranks – Mr Girl-Hunter. Whaaaat?! Here? Yes, and Miss Husband-Hunter, too! They like to think they are following Jesus whatever the cost. But really, they are following the twitterings of their own hearts. Mr Girl-Hunter meets a girl during the summer gospel crusade, and she says, 'I'm going on tour for a year.'

'My,' he said, 'isn't that a coincidence? The Lord has been leading me that way as well.'

He thinks he is following Jesus, but really he is following *her*. He is led astray by the deceitfulness of his own heart.

With Miss Husband Hunter, maybe it started back in her own church the first time she heard the work presented – when that good-looking young man got up and said, 'Come on tour for a year and serve the Lord.' It sounded so terrific . . . especially the way *he* said it! She thought (not consciously, of course), 'Well, maybe I'll never get a chance with him, but if there is one, there must be more.'

We are usually not aware of such thoughts because they occur in our subconscious minds. That is why God wants to shine the spotlight of His Word right down to the depths of our subconscious. That is why we must hide the Word in our hearts, study it, meditate on it, digest it; so that it might get down deep into the inner man – the real self.

God will not allow you to share your love for Him with anybody else, so make sure, young people, that you are following Jesus and not some fellow or girl. The Lord may give you a wife. Wonderful! He may give you a husband. Praise Him! The Bible says, 'The man who finds a wife finds a good thing' (Proverbs 18:22, Living Bible). But let it be God who brings you a husband or a wife, and not *you* who goes out looking for one! He is far more capable of choosing the one who is best for you than you are!

Mr Shortcut

The next pseudo-disciple to come along is Mr Short-cut. He truly has a vision for the mission field and wants to see the world bombarded with the gospel of Christ. He spots us through his binoculars, sees all these young people going off to evangelise, and he says, 'That's for me!'

He had thought about going to college . . . but oh, that takes four years! He had thought about Bible College, but it would take a chunk out of his life, and he is already 18. He has considered many things, but they all take so long and he just can't wait.

Operation Mobilisation seems to him the ideal thing – a shortcut to discipleship! A shortcut to world evangelism! But unfortunately the shortcut often turns out to be the longest road.

We must realise, young people, that there is no shortcut in accomplishing things for God. This has been our belief from the beginning of this work. Remember, this work is not a mission board, but a training programme meant to give experience and preparation to young men and women, so that after a couple of years (maybe even six or seven years), they can go out as missionaries, sent by their local assembly or church, or by some mission society.

Many young people who have been on previous crusades and have really understood the purpose of OM are now in university or Bible College. They discovered that one or two years with OM gives them something for which to work when they return to college or higher education.

I do not mean to imply by this that after OM everyone should return to college. Each person is different.

If we would only realise that you cannot put everyone in the same mould. The great cry today is, 'Everybody to Bible College.' *Druuummm, dum, dum!* Everybody off to Bible College like a bunch of tin soldiers. You just cannot serve Christ if you have not been to Bible College!!

I praise God that I graduated from one, but I certainly do not believe that everyone who wants to serve Christ *must* go to Bible College. I do believe that everyone who wants to serve Christ must go to *God*'s college, whatever it might be. It might be in the mechanic's shop or the literature department. It might be at the typewriter or in the kitchen. Or it might be learning at the feet of a man of God. This seems to me a bit more scriptural than some of the methods we are using today.

We must realise that there are no shortcuts to the kind of life that Jesus Christ meant for us. It is a long, hard road, and we are all just learners. Think of the Roman Catholic priest who studies nine years before he is ordained, or think of the medical student who studies for seven years before he can set up practice as a doctor, often postponing marriage and a home because medicine comes first. But we sometimes have a Mr Shortcut with us who feels that after one year with OM he is ready to turn the world upside down. Actually, he can hardly get up on time!

Mr Shortcut is a pseudo-disciple who is unwilling to pay the price and persevere. He is continually jumping from one place to another, and makes no impact anywhere. Young people, do not look for a shortcut. There is none for a life that is going to count. *Never sacrifice the permanent on the altar of the immediate.*

Mr Sluggard

Next we meet Mr Sluggard. Billy Graham names slothfulness as one of the seven deadly sins, and it is certainly one of the most common which I see in our day. Think of the prophet Nehemiah, and those people who 'had a mind to work' (Nehemiah 4:6) – where are this kind of men today? Think about the virtuous woman of Proverbs 31, who did her work early in the morning before anyone was up and was still going late at night by the light of her candle – where is this kind of girl today?

Proverbs 26:13 gives us a picture of the sluggard: 'The lazy man won't go out and work. "There might be a lion outside!" he says' (Living Bible).

Funny, isn't it? Now I don't think it is very likely that there really was a lion in the streets. The truth is, the man is lazy and sees only the obstacles.

You say, 'Let's press on.' But he says, 'Oh, we have to get our rest.' You say, 'Let's move out from house to house.' But he says, 'It's pretty cold today. We might catch cold.'

For every suggestion he has a 'But . . . if . . . no . . . can't.' He has ninety-nine negatives for every positive step forward, but the real problem is that he is lazy. Proverbs 20:4 says, 'The sluggard will not plow by reason of the cold.' I would like to paraphrase that verse: 'The OM'er will not go door to door by reason of the rain.' One sub-zero day in Austria the leader says, 'Let's go, troops, out on the doors!' Mr Sluggard begins shaking and quivering and says, 'Don't you think we should have a little extra Bible study today?' What a grievous thing it is when we use Bible study as an excuse for laziness. I see it all over the evangelical world.

The man in the secular world gets up at 6.30 a.m. and is on his job, working hard at 8.00 a.m. But the evangelical! Well, he is in 'full-time' Christian work and so he gets up at 7.30 or 8.00, has a leisurely breakfast, followed by a two-hour Bible study. Is this right, young people? To have a two-hour Bible study is an excellent plan *if* we are intensively studying with the purpose of letting the Word of God mould our lives. But it is *not* right if we are relaxing in our favourite armchair with our Bible in our hands, merely reading and lethargically looking out the window from time to time. Reading without taking notes is simply an invitation to sleep. Our Bible study should not be an ingenious subconscious excuse to get out of work – but rather an intensive, exhausting mental and spiritual experience! What an insult it is to God to fall asleep reading His Word! Can you imagine my sitting here face to face with Jesus Christ, and as He talks to me I begin to yawn and say drowsily, 'Isn't that tremendous, Lord?' . . . and then I fall asleep! And this is what happens. What mockery to God the way we sometimes have our quiet time. If you tend to grow sleepy during Bible study, try walking around and memorising a little. John Wesley used to study his Bible on horseback as he travelled across England from one open air meeting to another.

Look at Proverbs 20:13 – 'Love not sleep, lest thou come to poverty; open thine eyes, and thou shalt be satisfied with bread.'

We have been discovering that with a group as immature as we are, it is good to have to knock on doors, and 'keep going', carrying a heavy bookbag and earning our daily keep. It is the greatest tent-making business we can engage in. If the Apostle Paul was not ashamed to make tents and sell them, dare any of us be ashamed to go out and sell Christian books to earn at least a bit of our support, so that the few gifts that come our way can be channelled to more strategic people? – to those faithful Indians, Mexicans, Spaniards and Italians who can speak the language! Let *them* go out and do the personal work. Let *us* support them with our money and prayers!

God give us a vision for tent-making. Let us be zealous in all we attempt, and not be deceived into thinking that we are disciples when our life says we are sluggards.

Mr Little-As-Possible

Mr Sluggard has a very close friend, about whom I will say only a little. He is Mr Little-As-Possible. He rides into OM headquarters in the back of a truck, and is the first one out. Someone else will unload the truck and clean it out, so he goes and has a chat with his friends. Mr Little-As-Possible volunteers occasionally for the washing-up (especially when he sees that the girl he has his eye on has volunteered). But he only manages to get the plates and cups and cutlery washed. He puts the pots and pans to one side to soak and never remembers to wipe the crumbs off the table or clean the stove. If only we could exchange Mr Little-As-Possible for a Mr Much-As-Possible! Oh for some Extra-Mile men. These are the ones who do more than they are asked to do, and if they are not asked to do it, they do it anyway. These are the ones I want on my team. We have had them on our OM teams, many of them, and I tell you every one of them thrills my heart. They are a rebuke to my life.

Mr Halfway

But here comes another pseudo-disciple: Mr Halfway. He cannot wait – 'Let's go, start the race!' Vroommm! And he is off and away, ahead of everyone else. People look at him and think he is a sure winner – such energy, such speed. But halfway around the track he begins huffing and puffing and then, 'My, it's a long way to the end . . . just don't think I can make it. Maybe I've made a mistake?' And he comes to a grinding halt, and looks for another race.

Have you ever begun something you didn't finish? Silly question! We all have. It would be interesting to know how much money we invested last year in Navigator Courses for young people who had a great burst of zeal for Bible memorisation. Many of them are still on the second packet. It is false zeal, and when the energy of the flesh has exhausted itself, this zeal will be no more!

Miss Successful

Now let's meet Miss Successful. Her whole joy is in doing her job well, because when she completes it, it gives her a great feeling of accomplishment, and of course brings her recognition and praise as well.

Do you enjoy that feeling of accomplishment? Psychologists would say, 'Of course, it is necessary for human happiness and well-being. One who has no sense of accomplishment will end up in a mental home.' It is true that God often allows us to have a feeling of accomplishment, but unless we present the work accomplished to Him, and give Him all the glory for having enabled us to do it, then I am afraid that it will be included in the wood, hay, and stubble on the day of Judgment. It is self-produced zeal which so often works fervently, simply to be able to say, 'I have finished the job! I am a success!'

Miss Successful is at her best when others of the group are working close by, especially if a good-looking fellow is giving out tracts across the street from her. And, on her own for a day of book-selling, she put everything she has into it, and really excels. She feels terrific, just bubbling over with her success when she meets the group that evening. She is feeling so happy, in fact, she does not even realise how much all her glowing stories discourage the quiet girl on the team who has been faithfully knocking on the doors all day with no outward signs of success. In actual fact, young people, it is often this timid girl who has quietly committed her work unto the Lord who is the real Miss Successful, spiritually speaking.

Mr Know-It-All
and
Mr Teach-Me-Not

Next on the list are Mr Know-It-All and Mr Teach-Me-Not. These pseudo-disciples are very plentiful. Mr Know-It-All says, 'I know how to put that tent up. You just get out of the way a minute.' And his brother says, 'That's right. Look, you can't tell us anything about camping. We've done it all our lives. We have experience.' We often discover these twins among the older folk. Now, I am aware that the older generation feels that all the problems lie in us, and I think we realise that we are often guilty and must bend and break and repent. But, oh, how it thrills my heart to meet a pastor, an elder, a missionary who is willing to admit that he might be wrong, that there still might be one lesson he can learn before he gets to Glory – and who is humble enough to be willing to learn it from a young person, if God so desires. Believe me, I want to learn all I can while I am young, but if I live to be a hundred I want to keep on learning and bending and breaking until the day I go to meet my Lord.

These twins find their way on to almost all of the OM teams and make life generally unpleasant for the rest. I would be so happy to send them home where they would no doubt be appreciated for all their experience and knowledge. One thing is certain about them: they are sure to quench the Holy Spirit in their lives by their unteachable spirit.

Mr Noise-Maker

One pseudo-disciple who is just clamouring for acknowledgment is Mr Noise-Maker. You can usually find him in a prayer meeting, punctuating every other word with a constant stream of 'Amen's', 'Hallelujah's', etc. Now there is nothing wrong with a good shout of genuine praise (and we have probably more people on the other end of the pendulum who wouldn't let loose a shout of praise if they saw a man jump out of the grave!) but if you are a Mr Noise-Maker, you had better be careful, for God might just test the genuineness of your noise.

'Praise the Lord!' you shout when you find a pencil that you lost. What do you mean by that? Are you really offering praise to the Lord, or is it just a little

Christian slang expression you throw around lightly? 'Amen!' you say when someone prays, 'Lord, I believe you for five thousand souls this year in Italy.' Do you really believe it? Be careful what you 'amen' in a prayer.

Why, in some of our prayer meetings you can almost hear Satan's strongholds crumbling in the background, but then a month later, when there isn't quite the same 'atmosphere', when perhaps some discouragements have been experienced or you haven't heard any stirring messages recently, then when the time for the prayer meeting comes the only noise to be heard is the low moan of a group of discouraged little would-be Christian disciples. Let us be careful that our discipleship does not end with noise ... words ... sounds ... that fade away in the noise of battle.

Search your heart and count the cost until, by God's grace, you are convinced that when the day of trial and difficulty or heartache comes, you will be making the same noise! There is nothing wrong with a good shout, a good 'Amen!' But don't praise God only when you are 'on top'. Be prepared to praise Him just as much when you are down in the valley. He has not changed just because your spirits are low.

Mr Doctrine-Pusher

The next pseudo-disciple is rather stubborn – he is Mr Doctrine-Pusher. You are likely to meet Mr Noise-Maker pretty quickly but Mr Doctrine-Pusher is rather quiet at first, especially when someone is around who is well grounded in the Word. He comes out of his hiding once he has identified those hungry Christians who really want to get to know the Word more thoroughly. Then he begins to 'share' his views on the Word, and he comes up with some of the most interesting doctrines you have ever heard. He prefers to air his views behind the back of the leader, and most of all when he is alone with one or two weaker Christians. He quickly picks out the sincere ones who really want to learn more of God, and he is certain that he is the very one to teach them – he has just the hard core of truth that they need.

There are people who are close to being mentally ill on this point – you just cannot talk to them; you cannot reason with them; you cannot even get on the same wavelength with them. There are some heart-breaking cases of this type – people whose lives are so obviously a sham that everybody knows it, but when you begin to question them on their lives they begin to rave about their pet doctrines; they relate everything to these and nothing will deter them. Most people who get on some doctrinal tangent are people who have definite psychological problems. The mental institutions of the world are filled with deeply religious, but deceived people, who suffer from illusions of religious grandeur. But there are also many people like this who are not in institutions. Do not be surprised if you find one sitting next to you at church.

Some of the most fantastically fiery preachers I have ever heard in my life were in the southern part of the United States, raving and shouting about some religious obsession they had, and there are things that have been said on radio broadcasts along this line that would knock you off your chair. The United States has more sects and cults and false religions than most pagan countries in the world. There is every possible type of primitive, apostolic, sub-apostolic and super-apostolic group, and the followers of them are almost always absolutely convinced that they have the truth. We want no one like this on our teams – people who are determined to air their views and push their own doctrines; they are a hindrance.

Mr Sign-Seeker

The next pseudo-disciple is a close relative of Mr Doctrine-Pusher. His name is Mr Sign-Seeker. He can never make any decisions without having a definite 'sign' from God, and still worse, in every minor detail and circumstance of life he sees a 'sign'.

If the doorknob falls off in his hand, it is a sure sign from God that he shouldn't leave the house that day. When some nice boy happens to open the door for Miss Sign-Seeker, she is convinced that he is the one God has for her. If these sign-seekers go for an hour without selling a book, they say God has shown them that they should pack up and go home for the day. Mr Sign-Seeker always has some sensational new story to tell you, and he is usually an ardent follower of some of the spectacular 'sign-promoters' of our day. Frankly, it is a bit difficult for me sometimes to draw the line between 'sign' and just plain old superstition!

Beware, young people! The Lord Jesus said, 'A wicked and adulterous generation seeketh after a sign; and there shall no sign be given unto it, but the sign of the prophet Jonas' (Matthew 16:4).

The Lord Jesus did not want His disciples to seek after signs but after Himself; not after blessings but after the Blesser – Himself. Why, people will flock from all over the world to a convention when they are told they will receive a blessing. They will fly first class jet from California to New York to receive a blessing. But I have always wondered what would happen if one of these conventions put a sign up saying 'Suffering for all'. How many would attend then? And yet, doesn't the Word teach, 'For unto you it is given in the behalf of Christ, not only to believe on Him, but also to suffer for His sake' (Philippians 1:29)? May God search our hearts on this point.

Mr Worry-Wart

Next we meet Mr Worry-Wart. He is pressing on and really seems to be going places! He is often very diligent and conscientious, and to see his puckered brow you would think he is deep in thought. But really, he is deep in worry! He worries about whether he is good enough for God. He worries about whether he is accomplishing enough. He worries about getting his job done on time. He worries about his team members. He worries about the vehicles. He worries about opposition from the police. And on and on. And he thinks that worry is an essential part of his life – nothing will be accomplished if he does not worry about it.

But I want to tell you that worry is not a virtue, it is a sin! It is the sin which says, 'I don't trust you, God – I don't really believe you can take care of this problem. I don't really believe You have permitted this mistake for my good. I don't believe You are absolutely in control!'

The real problem is that Mr Worry-Wart has not learned to rest in Christ. Let us press on to learn this precious lesson.

Mr Adventurer

Have you met the next pseudo-disciple? He is Mr Adventurer. He is young and energetic, and when he hears about Operation Mobilisation it looks like the juiciest steak he has ever come across! He has the opportunity of crossing continents at 21 years of age! He can see the seven wonders of the world and take all kinds of slides and send them home to his friends, and learn languages and ride on camels and – oh, how exciting!

Oh dear, I feel so sorry for Mr Adventurer. He is one of the most disillusioned persons on OM. What he thinks is going to be a long, exciting holiday turns out to be a sort of 'pressure' cooker. True, he may go from England to India, but it will be in the back of a truck ... that has no windows ... and he will not be able to see anything all the way, except the faces of his teammates. If he sees the Taj Mahal at all, he will be giving out tracts so fast he will hardly notice it. And as for his little camera, well, he leaves that at home.

I can tell you, young people, it is no adventure to knock on doors in 120-degree heat all day long. He may think it is the first week, and the second and the third. But what about the second *month*? Soon Mr Adventurer will be asking for a trip home, tourist class. And we just do not bring them back from India so soon.

May God drive from us the spirit of adventure and make us count the cost. This is warfare! it will be hard from beginning to end. It will be against our flesh, our culture, our habits! Mr Adventurer needs to get off at the first stop.

Mr Freeloader

There is another pseudo-disciple who makes his way into Operation Mobilisation every year – Mr Freeloader. What? They don't even charge you to go on OM? That's for me!' And Mr Freeloader packs his bag and 'joins' OM.

He travels free, he always has at least a few square feet of floor space to sleep on, his meals are provided for him, and all his needs are met.

Yet, strangely enough, it is always a Mr Freeloader who is the first to complain when a vehicle breaks down or a meal is late. 'Terrible living conditions,' he says. 'Awful food. We should be having meat more often. Our bodies need it!'

He is one of those dual personalities and his other name is Mr Little-As-Possible. He has a very warped idea that, though he contributes nothing, he should still receive only the best.

Now, it is true that we do not require a tuition or anything in the way of money from you. But does that mean that you are not expected to contribute *anything? No!* This, of course, is grace. But I say to you that grace does over and above the minimum, and I am here to remind you that you are responsible before God to believe Him to supply your needs!

You may be young and weak in the faith and feel that you just cannot believe God for anything. But you must start somewhere, and if you just set a small amount before God that you can believe Him for, as He provides that, your faith will begin to grow. And I trust that what you cannot believe Him to supply in funds at first, you will make up in hard work and a disciplined life. Then, when God sees that you mean business about this, you will begin to see the funds come in.

The Bible says, 'If any would not work, neither should he eat.' Remember this, young people, and if you are not disposed to a hard day's work, then please, just do not appear at the meal table.

Oh, that God would put within all Christians a mind to work!

Mr Too-Busy

The next young pseudo-disciple is in such a hurry that we hardly have time to meet him! His name is Mr Too-Busy. He knows very little about real discipleship, but he manages to cover it all up with a very busy life. He likes to tell you how busy he is. 'Can't possibly do that, I'm too busy. I must get these letters written . . . no, first I'll make that telephone call . . . or should I first fill these book orders? Oh, dear, so much to do. And then George has asked me to do this and this and this for him . . . you must excuse me. I have to run.' And away he goes, Mr Too-Busy, like a whirlwind. He is blissfully ignorant that he is the poor victim of an undisciplined and sadly disorganised life. His problem is that he never sits down to organise his jobs and plan the way to accomplish them most efficiently. So he rushes around, unable to decide which are priority jobs and unable to give his full attention to any one of them. Despite his appearance of busyness, he actually accomplishes very little.

Now don't confuse Mr Too-Busy with Mr Busy. He too has many, many responsibilities, but he is able to take care of them with a minimum of noise and confusion. Both are active. Both walk quickly and have many things to do. But Mr Too-Busy is always confused and never completes one job without rushing hither and thither, getting more and more panicky as unresolved problems and difficulties pile up on him.

On the other hand, Mr Busy, although he is in a hurry, moves quickly but calmly, faithfully taking care of one responsibility as he acquires another.

Let us be careful to make this distinction, because we do not mind at all if Mr Too-Busy has a little more training in a secular job until he can learn to manage his time a little better. But we are always on the look-out for a Mr Busy on OM. I believe that the Spirit of God is desirous of moving us along in world evangelism at something more than a snail's pace, because at the present rate, beloved, we are going rapidly backwards in the job of reaching the world for Christ! Some of us need to learn to move a little faster, think faster, concentrate harder. Frankly, I get a little weary of being warned not to 'rush ahead of the Lord'. I believe that the disciples were in a hurry to get the job done. They were not in a panic, in a frenzy, in a mad rush. But, young people, they were moving – the book of Acts is the fastest-moving book in the New Testament. True, they waited on God (and much of their waiting they did at night, while our dear brethren – who like to give this advice today – get their regular eight hours of beauty sleep). But after they waited on God they moved out into action for Him. Let us beware of a life which is busy but barren. May we continue to strive for efficiency and speed in accomplishing our routine tasks for Him. Every minute we save in accomplishing these tasks is a minute we can spend in direct evangelism.

Mr Status-Seeker

And now, we will meet the last pseudo-disciple, Mr Status-Seeker. He is driven by a great desire for position and importance. He wants to be known as a man of God; he wants to be known as a great preacher, a great Bible teacher, a great organiser. He wants a special title which he can nail on the door of his private office. And it is all a sham to God. Recognition of man ... what is it? In the sight of God – nothing!

America is a nation of status seekers, and status seeking has so infiltrated American Christendom that we hardly know how to accept a person for what he is. And the majority of the world follows close behind in this frantic quest for recognition. The famous book, *The Status Seekers*, by Vance Packard, shows how the people of the world are status seekers. But how deadly it is when this same motivation comes into our Christian service. How often we treat a man kindly because we want something from him or because he has a certain status. How unreal that is – how God must hate it.

Young people, what are the titles given to the Lord Jesus Christ? Servant, Man of Sorrows, Man acquainted with grief, Foot-washer, Lamb of God. These are His titles. And His status symbol? Well, he never got a university degree. He didn't have a private office, nor a secretary, nor an expense account. No! His only status symbol was the Cross. Do you want more, young person? Do you feel a little out of place because you have no status, no official position? Do you want to stop being a 'nobody' and become a 'somebody'? Well, then, don't say you want to be a follower of Jesus, because He was a Somebody – but He became a Nobody! He, 'being in the form of God ... made

Himself of no reputation . . .' (Philippians 2:6, 7). Oh, may God deliver us from this curse of our day, this craving for recognition and praise of men. May our only claim be that we are 'accepted in the Beloved' (Ephesians 1:6).

Well, after all this, I can hear you saying to yourself, 'That finishes me. I'm going home. I realise I am a phony. Who can live up to that?'

Just a minute, please, and let me say this: Nobody can live up to it! *Nobody!* The only answer then is the all-sufficiency of Christ. Admit that you are a sinner. Admit that you are a failure. Come to the Cross of Christ and allow His life to take over in you. After all this you would think we would all be walking on the Calvary Road, wouldn't you? You would think we would be going to our friends, our wives, our husbands, our leaders, in brokenness and repentance. 'I lost my patience with you. I'm sorry. Please forgive me. . . . Look, brother, I shouldn't have said that. I've sinned against you.'

We are not going to have communion with God if we are always pretending, pretending, pretending, pretending. Why are we afraid to come to the light, to the Cross, to each other with our wretched sinful lives? It is our only hope! Do you know, after some messages, the ones who come to me in brokenness are the ones who are walking closest to the Cross! Often they are leaders in this work. I know they are living for the Lord. I know they are walking with Him . . . and yet they come in repentance because He has convicted them on some point or other in their lives. After the message on 'Hunger for God', I received a letter from one of the leaders who is probably doing more than most . . . and he was absolutely broken to tears and repentance.

Oh, for more like this! Men and women who will not harden their hearts, not even on some minor point, but will bend and break and walk in daily revival. If you have sinned against some brother, or offended him in any way, there is only one course for you and that is to go in humility and say, 'Forgive me.'

I pray that no one will go on from here without knowing the reality of being broken and cleansed before the Lord. You might be a leader, you might be a pastor. But I tell you, the only place of grace and blessing is at the foot of the Cross of Christ. He will cleanse you, and as you go out into this newness of life, whenever the Spirit speaks to you about something, whenever you find any of these twenty-one little men or women moving into your life, immediately you must repent and turn to Christ, and realise that He cleanses from these areas of sin. But do not hide it! Do not bury it! Do not let your pride keep you from confessing it. Let us stay at the foot of the Cross where the blood of Christ cleanses from all sin!

Extremism

The Holy Spirit was given to the church that we might be one, that we might love one another, that we might have a Comforter, a Teacher, a Counsellor, a Guide, and power in witness. Yet today the church is more divided over the doctrine of the Holy Spirit than one would dare to imagine.

For several years, I have been relatively silent concerning my personal views, because I wanted to avoid what I considered any unnecessary clash. I realise that what I am going to say could be taken in the wrong way by some. But I pray that all will face up to the tremendous problem which confronts us in this matter. To pretend that no problem exists is neither practical nor realistic.

The problem is a very real one, especially when members of two churches of different denominations do not so much as speak to one another because of this doctrine.

The problem exists in Britain, in America, on the Continent, and indeed everywhere we go. I believe that God wants to keep us above this controversy and to use the unity of the Spirit to confound the attempts of the devil to bring strife and division.

Rather than present only my own beliefs, I want to examine three of the main streams of thought concerning the Holy Spirit. It is the third that I especially want to expose as false and dangerous.

The First Group

The first school of people are those who lean, to a greater or lesser degree, toward what is called Calvinistic theology. It is impossible to fit everyone into a strict category, as most of us have elements from differing schools of theology. But in general, these groups tend to emphasise the Sovereignty of God and the eternal security of the believer.

Concerning the Holy Spirit, a distinction is made between the 'baptism of the Spirit', which they believe occurs simultaneously with conversion, and the 'filling of the Spirit', which is after. Both experiences are for all believers. They believe, furthermore, that one is filled with the Spirit through yielding his life to Jesus Christ. They would not eliminate crisis experiences (and many have had them), but they would put a heavier emphasis on being filled daily with the Spirit and on walking in the Spirit. Of course, among these people there are many different ideas about the Holy Spirit and sanctification.

McConkey's book, *The Threefold Secret of the Holy Spirit*, Emmaus Bible Correspondence Courses, and many other books written by leading men, are strong in the above-mentioned emphasis.

The Second Group

The second school is that which leans toward Arminian theology. Again, most people do not fit strictly into this category. These groups, generally speaking, emphasise more the free will of man and the possible loss of salvation through sin. They emphasise what is called the 'second blessing' or the 'baptism of the Spirit'. Many people within these groups believe that the Holy Spirit indwells a person at the time of his conversion, but the general teaching is that a person needs a definite experience of sanctification or 'second blessing' and that it is through this experience that he receives power for service and for ministry.

There is great variance in what the different groups actually mean by these terms. Some men from, say, a strong Methodist school, preach a tremendous message on sanctification and the baptism of the Spirit . . . but there is great difference between what they mean by these terms and what, perhaps, the Pentecostals mean, though the two groups are in the same general school of theology.

These, then, are the two basic schools of theology today: those leaning toward Calvinism, with a heavy emphasis on the Sovereignty of God, on progressive sanctification, and eternal security; and those leaning towards Arminianism, with a stronger emphasis on the free will of man, the baptism of the Spirit, and the possibility of 'falling from grace'.

As I said before, do not attempt to place everyone into one of these two schools, for you will never do it. Most of us have been influenced to some extent by both schools of thought.

Great Men

From both schools have come great men of God: Jonathan Edwards, for instance, leaned heavily towards Calvinism, while Charles Finney leaned more strongly towards Arminianism. George Whitefield leaned towards Calvinism, but John Wesley towards Arminianism. Hudson Taylor leaned towards Calvinism whereas General William Booth towards Arminianism, and on we could go giving a great list of hundreds of names of men from both schools. All lived lives in the power of the Holy Spirit. We can see that whether they believed in the 'second blessing', or whether they believed in a continual filling of the Spirit, the lives of one group were as powerful as the other group. Now this is the tremendous thing! We must constantly remember that the committed and dedicated lives of men in one school of theology are as powerful as the lives of committed men from the other school. I could name man after man who has never experienced a 'special' baptism of the Spirit, who has never claimed a 'second blessing', and yet whose life has been filled with the power of the Holy Spirit, as he has daily sought to live in the Spirit, yielding to Him. I could name many, also, who have claimed to have experienced the baptism of the Holy Spirit. I wish we could have a few Wesleys now, or Whitefields. You could give me a Calvinistic Whitefield or an Arminian Wesley to work with. I can work with any man, if only he has such reality in his life.

Many people know that I personally lean towards the Calvinistic school of theology. But I have learned a great deal from Christians in the other school. I think *Herald of His Coming* is a tremendous paper and we distribute it widely, though it isn't exactly Calvinistic, to say the least! I read literature produced by both schools, and we have distributed the book, *Why Revival Tarries*, which is a product of the Arminian group.

I was recently reading a book about the Holy Spirit which was produced by the Arminian school. The author said that when a man is baptised with the Holy Spirit he will manifest the fruit of the Spirit. If he doesn't, then it is all noise, and the so-called baptism experience is of no value. This illustrates the fact that the greater controversies have often come among people who are actually in the same schools, leading to even more and more divisions. In Ephesians 5:18, we are told 'be filled with the Spirit'. In Galatians, we are told what the results of such a filling will be: love, joy, peace, long-suffering, gentleness, goodness, faithfulness, meekness, and temperance. Without the fruit of the Spirit manifest in the life, all claims to any kind of 'experience' are spurious and invalid.

As you look today for people who are truly showing forth the fruit of the Holy Spirit, you need a good magnifying glass! I believe that all men of all schools of theology will agree that we must have the fruit of the Spirit manifest in our lives.

I once underlined every verse in the New Testament in which the fruit of the Spirit is mentioned, and I discovered that one or more is mentioned on almost every page of the New Testament. Fruit is emphasised hundreds and hundreds of times.

I believe that here we need to make an important distinction between the fruit of the Spirit and the gifts of the Spirit. The fruit of the Spirit is produced in *all* Christians as they yield to the Holy Spirit. The gifts, however, are given according to the will of God. He may bestow one gift upon one individual and half a dozen gifts upon another according as He sees fit ... but the ninefold fruit is produced in every Spirit-controlled life.

There is a great trend today to over-emphasise the gifts of the Spirit, especially one or two of the gifts. There is always a great danger in such over-emphasis of any truth of the Word for it is very easy to become a 'Johnny-one-note', not giving other truths the emphasis they require to produce balanced living.

I do not pretend here to give a message on the gifts of the Spirit, for that is far beyond the scope of this short message. But I want to look for a moment at 1 Corinthians 12, concerning the gifts of the Spirit. In verses 8–11, we read, 'For to one is given by the Spirit the word of wisdom; to another the word of knowledge by the same Spirit; to another faith by the same Spirit; to another the gifts of healing by the same Spirit; to another the working of miracles; to another prophecy; to another discerning of spirits; to another diverse kinds of tongues; to another the interpretation of tongues: but all these worketh that one and the self-same Spirit, dividing to every man severally as *He will*.' Not necessarily as we might desire! The gifts are given as *He wills*.

We read in 1 Corinthians 12:28, 'And God hath set some in the church, first apostles, secondarily prophets, thirdly teachers, after that miracles, then gifts of healings, helps, governments, diversities of tongues.' The gift of *helps*! This is probably the least sought-after of all the gifts today! Yet if there were a few more people around with the gift of 'helps' we would probably see far greater unity and effectiveness in the work of the Lord.

And God's *Word* says: 'Are all apostles? Are all prophets? Are all teachers? Are all workers of miracles? Have all the gifts of healing? Do all speak with tongues? Do all interpret? But covet earnestly the best gifts: and yet show I unto you a more excellent way.'

Sometimes when I see how Christians grasp for certain gifts of the Spirit, I am reminded of how children all grab for the biggest package under the Christmas tree. How very selfish we all are by nature!

Spiritual Gifts

In marked contrast to this, I can never forget the words of a dear brother in the Lord who has had much influence on my life. How it spoke to my heart when he prayed and really meant it, that I be given the better blessing. He prayed that if either of us were to be married, and if there was a wife for only one of us, that I would be the one to get the wife! He later ushered at my wedding, still single, and how it impressed me, when instead of crawling after the blessing like so many of us, he had prayed that the other fellow might be blessed!

Granted, a wife is not exactly in the realm of spiritual gifts, but I wonder how many times we get on our faces and really and honestly seek that the others might be given spiritual gifts? There is a rat-race in the twentieth century to get the gifts.

It is very interesting to note that the gift of tongues is never *mentioned* in any of the other epistles written to the churches. It is obviously that this gift was not evident in all the churches, and that is why it is so dangerous today for a church or group to judge or classify as 'unspiritual' a church or group where this gift is not in operation. It would be just as if the Corinthian church which had plenty of problems might judge the Ephesian church or Colossian church or the Thessalonians for not having the gift of tongues.

Now there are all sorts of interpretations as to what, exactly, these gifts constitute. And so again we move into controversial areas. The problem really boils down to the fact that those who are convinced one way are often so dogmatic that they can tolerate no other opinion. Let us take care that we are not so fixed and dogmatic in our minds concerning these points (which are not cardinal doctrines of the faith) that we feel we must, at all costs, convince others that our views are right.

Most of us are very young in our understanding of the Scriptures. Most of us are quick to form opinions, often without basis, and moreover, easily vacillate in our opinions. We have not the 'background' of theologians, most of whom study at least seven years, full-time! Many of us have not even been Christians for many years – to say nothing of having made concentrated studies of the Scriptures! How, then, can we think that with our little bit of hit-and-miss studying (or even with some systematic study) we have the answers to all these things that even the great men of God have not agreed upon? And in any case, even years of study does not give us the right to force our ideas on other people.

There is an unfortunate tendency among some of us to 'look down' upon theology and theologians. It is true that there are many students of theology who never get beyond theory in their studies, and many who embrace modernistic theology. Nevertheless, the study of theology itself is not to be contemptuously dismissed. Theology means the 'study of God'. I have heard some young people say, 'I don't need any theology.' How ridiculous! They 'don't need' to study about God? What they mean (I hope) is that they don't need any false theology or any modernistic theology. But don't say you don't need any theology. There is always a real danger when we move into unfamiliar areas and try to form opinions on scanty knowledge and meagre evidence. Some of our biggest problems come with young people who have their favourite verses – and with these verses can prove dogmatically anything they like. This can happen when discussing the subject of the Holy Spirit. We have met a number of people who could tell you anything you wanted to know about the Holy Spirit from their five favourite little verses – mostly out of context. There is a great danger in taking verses out of context (as is the case with such groups as the Jehovah's Witnesses and the Mormons) in order to thrust particular doctrines upon other people.

The Extremists

Now this brings us to the third group of people. *These are the extremists . . . or the 'ultras'!*

The *'ultras'* are those who get something good (or something bad) and *bang!* they go right to the extreme. The Calvinist believes in the Sovereignty of God. But extreme Calvinists (or Ultras) believe in the Sovereignty of God to such an extent that they take away completely the free will of man, and liquidate evangelism, seeing no need for zeal in witnessing or soul-winning.

'You don't need evangelism,' they say, 'if God wants to save the heathen, He will save them . . . don't you get excited about it. The whole world is in His hands.' True, God is sovereign over the world and the universe. But the place He most wants to be sovereign over is your heart, your life, your thoughts and actions.

Another group of Ultras are the Exclusive Brethren. You have no doubt read the newspaper stories of the way the strange doctrines of this group have split families, isolated the members of the group, and generally brought reproach to the Name of Christ. But did you know that this group was founded on some tremendous doctrines and some of the original men in the movement were strong, sound Bible teachers? Yet, somehow, they skidded off into tangents, further and further from the Truth – until today they have degenerated into what I would consider a sect.

Fortunately, with the Exclusive Brethren, there is not too much of a problem, simply because they are 'exclusive'! In other words, they keep to themselves. They go off into their corner, lock their doors, and you don't have to worry about them making much of an impact. They are a diminishing group. Many are going into other churches, or just leaving the faith altogether.

Over the Fence

On the other side of the 'theological fence' there are other groups of Ultras. There is a movement today known as the Neo-Pentecostal or Charismatic Movement, and there are some very good and balanced people among them. However, there are also many Ultras and extremists that often bring division and confusion and who often also tend to pull away from the main line of evangelical thinking into various kinds of splinter groups. This group often criticises the older Pentecostal denominations, and lately some Pentecostal leaders have also written materials warning people about the Neo (or 'New') Pentecostals. We find, however, that there are balanced and extreme people in both groups and this creates a situation that demands much wisdom, prayer and discernment.

One summer, for example, two young girls on an evangelistic team decided that the other girls on the team needed to have what they called the 'baptism of the Holy Spirit'. These girls, who were young and not well taught, began to meet with the other girls, encouraging them to seek the 'baptism of the Spirit'. The meetings took place late at night when they should have been sleeping. This situation greatly upset most of the girls on the team and began to cause division. Soon I began to hear all kinds of echoes of the incident.

When these girls were asked why they had broken the rule against riding a doctrinal hobby-horse in this way, indeed, why they had come on the team at all, one of them said that the team provided a way for her to get to that particular country. She wasn't really convinced on what was presented in the orientation sessions. She wasn't really united with the team, but apparently she had received some sort of vision about that land and thought that since this particular fellowship had vehicles, she would just go along! Well, you know, I do not feel that this was exactly God's method of leading her to that land. Nor do I accept her as a truly Spirit-filled person.

Day by Day

Many Christian leaders could testify to problems on their teams caused by the Ultra-Pentecostals – and I mean problems! These things happen when people move off on a tangent and begin to ride a doctrinal hobby-horse, and it simply cannot be tolerated in our work. We have tried to be nice, we have tried to be gentle, but we feel we must also be firm. It is a miracle the way our young people from many churches and backgrounds have worked together in unity for over 15 years, with almost no serious division. Truly, only the Holy Spirit of God can accomplish this miracle; and this, of course, was the greatest exhortation of Paul to the Corinthians, as we see in 1 Corinthians 1:10. I am one hundred per cent for miracles and Holy Spirit revival, but I believe it must be on God's terms and in God's timing. I am fully convinced that it must start in my daily life and in yours. I don't believe that revival consists merely of meetings, or noise, or emotional experiences. It is basically nothing more and nothing less than the life of Christ being lived out through each one of us day by day. We, of course, strongly believe that people should daily be filled with the Holy Spirit as we are commanded in Ephesians 5:18, which literally means 'be being filled' continuously.

I've heard so much about the Welsh Revival. I've been in Wales, and have spoken with men who witnessed the Welsh Revival. As far as I'm concerned, the Revival was cut off far short of its fulness. It is true that God gave them the initial passion, fervour, love and power. God brought hundreds to Himself. But when it should have led to militant discipleship and world evangelism, the fire was put out, and every possible sort of confusion and back-sliding resulted.

At about the same time as the Welsh Revival, one of the most militant missionary programmes the world has ever known was emerging in America; that of the

Missionary Alliance. They were ploughing on, reaping thousands of souls, under the direction of men who had more missionary vision that most of us will ever have. Then extreme teachings on the Holy Spirit, and the gifts of the Spirit, split them right down the middle and they have never been the same since. Other movements have been stopped or split over similar controversies. You can be sure the devil is usually behind it. The amazing thing is that some of the greatest divisions come among those who consider themselves 'more spiritual'.

Demons

I have met young people who are very young in the Lord and who are certainly anything but scholars of the Word. Nevertheless, somehow, they think they can begin to cast out demons. Every time they see a sick person they think, 'Demons!' We have heard young people on visits to the sick say, 'There's a demon in you. We must get the demon out.' And the poor patient nearly has a nervous breakdown! I have known people who, anytime they see something rather strange, say immediately, 'Demons!' This is, of course, an extreme viewpoint, but it is not uncommon. Now if you see someone who is truly demon-possessed, the thing to do is to fast and pray and take counsel with an older, more mature person. Do not feel you personally must rescue every person with deep problems. The biggest proof of your own immaturity and superficiality is to talk about it to individuals or little groups and to start rumours.

I know a mature man of God, a physician who has been mightily used to restore people and to pray for the sick. But he has the greatest hesitancy when it comes to moving in the area of demons. This is one of the most difficult of all ministries. I have no doubt that demons can be cast out, but I tell you, this is a job for mature men of God, men who have been anointed of God ... not children, like most of us. I have seen young people who have never led five people into an intimate relationship with Jesus Christ, who can't trust the Lord for 50p, but who propose to cast out demons! Believe me, these fellows are deluded.

I want to tell you with all seriousness that our mental institutions are jammed with religious people. Religious mania is classified by psychologists as an extremely fast-growing illness. And it comes from various extreme positions concerning religious matters. Actually people with certain kinds of emotional problems easily become extreme and fanatics. We praise God, however, for His grace to deliver such people, and this seems to have become to some degree one of our ministries over these years. Some people who were extreme for one reason or another have been attracted to our work, yet through the movement have come into a more balanced and loving, biblical position, theologically and emotionally.

Visions

We sometimes have people who get 'guidance' from God through visions and dreams, and we have a terrible time trying to counsel them. It's like trying to counsel a rock! You cannot budge them because God 'has spoken'. Look! God's method of guidance is the Word of God. I don't doubt that in some very special case He may give a vision to someone ... but that vision *must* be in accord with the Word of God. Usually other responsible brethren will recognise its genuineness. Extremist groups are often 'led' by women who declare emotional impulses as 'Thus saith the Lord'. But it is difficult to reconcile this method of guidance with the teaching of the Word.

Don't Trust Feelings

I have seen so much nonsense in this area. When I was much younger in the Lord, a girl told me that she had had a vision about the Philippines. God just 'picked her up bodily one night and laid her out on the floor and told her she was going to be a nurse in the Philippines'. Being so young in the Lord, I thought it was tremendous and began to pray for her. But three months later the vision had disappeared, she got married and went to California, where she has been living ever since. Was that a vision from God? Her brother had a similar experience – then got married, and a year later was divorced! Don't tell me that such visions come from God! Many extremist groups are plagued by various forms of immorality and even at times they defend this as spiritually 'pure love', quoting verses on 'body ministry' to defend their case. How important it is to realise that when we start taking verses out of context we can defend almost anything. Extremist groups and false cults often know very little about real biblical truth.

In Latin America, one particular extreme movement is absolutely torn by immorality, and I am speaking from evidence gained from sound investigations. The biggest reason is that most people in this group have an extreme trust in emotions and feelings. No matter what you are doing, you are in trouble when you begin to live lies and trust in your feelings. God said that we are to love Him with all our heart, soul, mind and strength. This includes the emotions, naturally, but it also includes the intellect (that is your faculty for reason and common sense), and these must work in accord with what God has set forth in His Word. When you begin to trust your inconsistent and unreliable feelings, you are in grave danger.

We must remember that the Holy Spirit is basically *Holy*! He is never just a spirit. It sometimes happens that those who are intent on seeking 'the Spirit' overlook that fact; that the Third Person of the Godhead is *Holy*. And herein is great danger. For in laying ourselves open to the spirit world, it is essential to recognise the fact that there is only one *Holy Spirit*, but there are multitudes of evil spirits. God says in 1 John 4:1, 'Beloved, believe not every spirit, but try the spirits whether they are of God.'

There have been meetings where people, seeking climactic, emotional experiences, have called for the Holy Spirit to come upon them. First, they were 'singing in the spirit', then 'praying in the spirit'. (This was good.) Then they were 'dancing in the spirit' and before the night was over men and women were actually engaging in gross immorality 'in the spirit'. The great question is, of course, which spirit? Beloved, Satan is an enemy! Don't ever forget it. Since this message was first given, a helpful book by a Pentecostal leader has been published, entitled *Queer Christians*. This book gives valuable information in regard to extremist tendencies and especially how immorality often works its way into such situations. Satan will try to take the best things and channel them into sordid ends. He will, if he can, take the sound doctrines of assemblies and turn them into extreme 'exclusive' doctrines. He will take the sound teachings on the Holy Spirit and twist them to an extreme, leading men into the depths of moral degradation.

He will try to take our Christian organisation, too, and make it extreme on some point or the other. He will try to make us 'discipleship thumpers', for instance, so that everywhere we go we'll thump 'discipleship'. And if we see someone with a diamond ring (or two pairs of shoes, or six dresses), we will say, 'Aha! A materialistic Christian!' There is a danger of our becoming so extreme that everyone 'must drain their bank account and forsake all'. I tell you, 'forsaking all' is mentioned more times in the Bible than the pet doctrines of these extreme groups. *But anything*, no matter how good, taken to an extreme, becomes a snare. Even prayer. Think of the monks and flagpole sitters who devoted so much time to prayer that they had to retire from society altogether, in order to have an uninterrupted prayer life.

Throughout Church history we find that many, many points of doctrine, good in themselves but carried to an extreme, have become heresies.

There are some controversial groups with whom we do not co-operate. I do not say they are not being used of God ... perhaps they are, I don't know. But it grieves my heart to see some sensational publicity programmes which consume millions of pounds yearly just on very biased, denominational type magazines (though they don't call themselves 'denominations') for Christians. Hundreds of magazines are prepared for Christians by these groups, pushing their pet doctrines ... and half the world goes to sleep tonight (hundreds of them never to wake again) having never received so much as a single Gospel tract!

One idea prevalent in some of these magazines and groups is that 'all sickness is of the devil'. This is another extreme viewpoint, which is, I believe, anti-scriptural. I know that God can heal the sick. I know that He can raise the dead! I believe God can do anything! I personally have seen sick people raised back to health after praying for them. Praise God! It isn't sensational; it doesn't require that I write a dozen magazine articles about it. What grieves me most about some of these groups is that every time someone is healed you see photos and illustrated articles splashed all over the place, and the glory is not primarily to God. I believe that great miracles, without great ethics, leads to great delusion.

Now, let's get to the core of the matter. We all agree that the one essential is that an individual be born again. Some people have tremendously emotional conversions. Others have had quiet conversion experiences. Some did not feel anything in particular, perhaps are not even sure of the exact time of their conversion.

Are those in the first category going to say that those in the second group have never been born again? Of course not! We can see very clearly that God sometimes works like a mighty rushing wind, and sometimes like a still, small voice. But in both instances, the important thing to remember is that God is working. God works in different ways in different people.

Now we pass from the conversion experience to sanctification. This is the big area of controversy. In much study, and through experience with hundreds of people, I have discovered that the important thing is not whether you have had a thunderbolt experience or a 'still, small voice experience'. I am not concerned what vocabulary you use ... whether you call it the 'baptism of the Spirit', 'the deeper life', 'a Keswick experience', or something else. The important point is: where are you *today* in terms of holiness. Is the fruit of the Holy Spirit manifest in your life each day, and to an increasing degree?

Some of the most dynamic, powerful, loving, Spirit-filled Christians I have ever met have never had a particular crisis experience. Who are we to say that an individual must have a certain type of experience in order to be Spirit-filled? It is very foolish, indeed, for a few extreme zealots to try to lead others into a particular experience. Our pushing an experience, instead of exalting Christ, leads many into confusion. Some even fake an experience in order to be accepted by some 'spiritual group'.

Taking a Stand

If you have had a crisis experience with the Lord, praise God! May He give you abundant power and fruit that remains. We praise God for you.

God's Word says we are to esteem our brother as better than ourself. Do you really esteem those who hold convictions different from yours, as better than yourself ... or do you feel that you must push your convictions upon them? If we cannot accept our brother as he is, and esteem him as better than ourself, then how in the world are we going to live together and work together? We can disagree on secondary matters and still have fellowship with one another.

I believe that most of us see the problem and are

willing to steer clear of controversial issues and to esteem the other man as better than ourselves. But if you are in the outer fringe of either of these groups, if you are an ultra (and I don't care what kind of ultra), if you feel that you must talk about your convictions to little groups, or that you must be on the lookout for individuals whom you can 'indoctrinate' . . . *then I beg of you not to join an evangelistic team* where you would only cause trouble and division. You will not be happy with the team, and the team will not be happy with you.

This does not mean that we do not love you; for this is our greatest burden, but though the Scripture teaches us to love everyone, it does not teach that we can work together in fellowship with everyone. We do not want to see the work of God divided and hindered by a few people who feel they must push their opinions and favourite doctrines, and feel they must share these things or else they would be compromising their faith. I believe this is just another subtle trick of Satan, for we do not find any such teaching in the New Testament. To try to keep the unity of the Spirit and emphasise the major truths of the Word of God is to put the most important doctrine in the Bible into practice – the doctrine of loving one another. How constantly we need to remind ourselves that without this we are merely sounding brass and tinkling cymbals. Perhaps we should all read 1 Corinthians 13 every day for one year, especially if we are the type of person who easily slides off on a side road.

God has said, 'Be ye filled with the Spirit', and as we yield ourselves to Him, He will fill us, whether we have a great emotional experience or whether we have a quiet, daily infilling. And when this happens in our ranks, the world is going to shake! When the world sees Anglicans working together with Pentecostals and Brethren, and loving one another, they will say, 'See how they love each other!' And they will know that we are disciples of Christ, for our Lord Himself said, 'By this shall all men know that ye are My disciples, if ye have love one to another' (John 13:35). It is this which will bring people into a realistic experience with Jesus Christ.

*   *   *

Recently, several of us went to Hyde Park, London, to preach in the open air. There was a big crowd there, and we got a box and stood up on it, and I began to preach. A crowd of 100 or more was milling around as I began. There were blacks, whites, Indians, Pakistanis and others among the crowd of onlookers. I spoke as a 'white' person. When I finished, my friend, who was black, stood up and spoke. There was absolute silence, and the people really listened. This crowd had read newspaper headlines about racial discrimination around the world. They had watched race riots on television and they carried in their minds the idea that blacks and whites just don't get on together, but here we Christians stood together, not only black and white, but people of every denomination, background, and nation, having in fact been working together for more than 15 years. Those onlookers could see that we loved each other, that we respected each other and that truly there was something real binding us together. They heard that it was the Lord Jesus Christ.

When Europe and Asia begin to see, with their own eyes, Christians from different cultures and different backgrounds 'getting on the same box', loving and re-specting one another – then they will begin to take notice! May God grant us the wisdom and the power to realise this, and to apply it to our lives.

Revolution of Balance

Spiritual balance is something that must be real for each one of us. If one only understands the principles superficially then he will quickly find that they will not stand the test of the secular world. It is my deep conviction that discipleship is not just for full-time workers. Discipleship is for every believer. Discipleship is not just for people who are living in a Christian fellowship. It is for people everywhere. Discipleship is not a set of rigid rules. The principles of discipleship are more flexible and adaptable than many of us would dare to admit. One set of Bible truths taken to extreme without the balancing truths of another set can lead people into frustration. Frustration will never lead to spiritual reality. I really want us to have a balance in our spiritual truth. I feel a great sense of failure that at times I have not had the courage to speak boldly what I believe the Bible teaches in some areas. I want us to look together at certain truths that are deeply embedded in my heart.

Groups Outside

Have strong convictions, but be flexible and adaptable as a person. The disciple, though he has strong convictions, is flexible and adaptable. His cardinal rule is *love*. When he goes into a situation with which he disagrees violently on some secondary matter and wants to war and stamp his feet and cry out and preach, love restrains him. Love should cause him to think before he speaks. Most of us realise our tongues run faster than our brains, and this gets us into much difficulty. The true disciple, though he has strong convictions, is adaptable and flexible.

Sometimes messages you hear build up strong convictions on minor issues as well. If you associate with another group, you may find they have different convictions. Unless you are flexible, adaptable and loving, you will not be able to fit into another fellowship easily.

Several times I have thought I would like to work with the Salvation Army. They are about as different in certain areas as any group can be from my basic beliefs. Yet, reading about them gave me a great desire to work with them, in spite of the areas in which I would not agree.

There is nothing wrong with a strong conviction if you realise you are a learner. Without that flexibility and adaptability, your convictions will dig your own grave. This is particularly true in the tough secular world.

Many missionary societies take offerings and make their financial need known. I have a strong conviction in the opposite direction. But, if God wanted me to join a group that believed this, then it would be possible, because of my conviction, although very strong, would be flexible. There are many examples of godly men who believed differently. William Booth took money from the unconverted and said, 'I will wash it in the tears of the widows and they will use it for the glory of God.' D. L. Moody said, 'The Devil has had it long enough, I will take it and use it for the glory of God.' God uses men of completely opposite convictions. There is one man of God who is a well known author. He visited us on the ship and during his sermon smoked a pipe all the time. Although he believes and acts differently, he is a man who is being wonderfully used of God. God is so great and so mighty, that He wants to work, and is going to use people despite their mistakes, their weaknesses, and even minor false doctrines and ideas. You can say at times, 'Others may, I cannot.' This is far better than saying, 'I cannot, therefore others may not', for this means that if they do then I will judge them.

High Aims

Have high goals, yet accept yourself completely. Many messages have been given on the subject of self-acceptance, although they may have been called different things. Yet it is very easy for us not to remember or even to grasp the message though we have heard it a number of times. The devil is a specialist in deceitfulness. The tendency is for us to judge others, to see the faults in others rather than in ourselves. When we hear powerful messages we tend to see the weaknesses in other people and to think we ourselves are doing fairly well, when this is not so.

We may have higher goals in some respects than some other Christian groups. These goals can make us into neurotics. Some Christians become neurotics because they aim at impossible standards. Christians tend to aim and accept fantastic goals that either kill them or so distress and discourage them that they backslide.

With our high goals and high aims we must have complete self-acceptance. We must have that deep inner peace because we are accepted in the Beloved, even when we are grovelling in the mud because of our own mistakes. It is a difficult balance to find and there is a great danger of neurosis.

We must have high goals. Let us aim high. Mr Fred Jarvis says, 'The great sin of Christians is not failure, but aiming too low.' We should aim as high as we can. We must aim high with complete self-acceptance; then, when a mistake is made we do not heap self-pity on ourselves and drown in the mire of discouragement and despair, but rather maintain a true spiritual balance.

The Discipline of Rest

The third spiritual balance is to have strong discipline while being relaxed and rested. It is important to be strong in both areas. There must be times when you throw yourself into difficult situations, releasing the greatest amount of energy and discipline, and there must be times when you throw yourself into being carefree and relaxed, floating on top of the world. Without both of these seeming extremes you are not going to make it.

Some will ask, 'Are we not supposed to be soldiers all the time?' Yes, but even a soldier does not keep his finger on the trigger all the time. A real soldier is a man who knows how to relax. When he relaxes he builds up his physical strength and power so he can go on to battle and accomplish more in a week than he would have done in a month. Billy Graham recently stated that if he could live the last 10 years of his life over again he thinks he would give himself completely to the battle and then retreat, giving himself to the Word, prayer and rest. Some think they should never take a holiday, should never relax for a moment, but this is not true. We must take it easy at times. A violin player tightens up his strings before playing a concerto, but when it is over he releases them or they would snap. In other words, we should learn to come apart or we will literally *come apart*.

For our health, as well as our spiritual life, it is important to learn to relax. Different people do this in different ways. Some people need complete separation from work to relax. Some need a week's holiday, and others can just take off a few hours, or even change their job and be relaxed. Other people's attitude towards their work enables them to work in a relaxed way and never become as up-tight as some others. Because we know so little of relaxation you will hear me preach more on the rest of faith than on discipline, though I believe in both equally.

When we come into the rest of faith our discipline will increase and not lessen. It is easy to produce a false discipline, following certain routines, because this is what the leaders expect. This is pseudo-discipline, something we want to drop.

It is self-discipline that remains, not enforced discipline. There will be many failures, but I know of no better way of learning than through failure. Yet in God's work the willingness to accept certain forms of external discipline is part of self-discipline. Let us aim for strong discipline yet be relaxed and rested in every situation.

Concentration Without
Frustration

Fourthly, we need concern without neurosis. Recent studies suggest that evangelical Christians with a strong Protestant outlook tend towards neurosis. There is a book written about neurosis in the church. It is healthy to have a concern that things are done right and people are living right without becoming neurotic. Let's have peace within ourselves when other things are going wrong. Having a sort of itch, a psychological compulsion which does not come from above but from one's ego, is neurosis. Actually we should not be afraid of a little bit of neurosis, and in fact most of us have some. The modern psychologists suggest we throw away our Protestant ethic with ideas such as, 'You can't have sex before marriage' because this makes us neurotics. But, as another psychiatrist recently stated, 'The Victorian ethic has produced a generation of neurotics and the twentieth century liberty ethic is producing a generation of psychotics.' A psychotic is ten times worse than a neurotic. We should be neither.

It is important to keep our rooms clean and tidy. If someone sees rubbish lying around, it is good to get rid of it. However, the neurotic is bothered if there is one speck of dust. He will not be able to live very easily anywhere because he is so bothered about getting rid of all the tiny specks of dust. Eventually he will burn up inside and continually move around, unable to settle at anything because of his neurosis. (This is often true in marriage also.)

Many perfectionists have neuroses. In the book, *None of These Diseases*, we see this brought out clearly. Perfectionists crack or else cause a lot of other people to crack.

God wants us to have concern and compassion, but not neurosis. Look at how the Lord Jesus humbled his stumbling, fumbling disciples. They said and did many stupid things, but He did not hate them. He rather forgave them, and even when He was nailed to the cross He said, 'Father, forgive them; for they know not what they do.' What an example this should be for us.

A true disciple or a balanced Christian is a man with unlimited forgiveness because he has Christ in the heart and Christ is unlimited forgiveness. The man who is ready and able to forgive easily and quickly can never become a neurotic, but he can still have a strong and real concern.

Perfection Through Failures

Fifthly, our goal is perfection while learning to handle shortcomings and failures. To be perfect should be the goal of every true Christian: to live a life in the Spirit, not to offend anyone, to have maximum love, to do all things right and to glorify God in every action. This is spiritual perfection and this should be our goal.

Each of us must come to a place where we are able to accept failure, especially our own failures, mistakes and shortcomings. Often the Christian has such high standards for himself that when he misses the mark he doesn't know what to do. He becomes so totally frustrated that he wallows in self-pity and takes a long time to get back to the beginning again. He will repent, he will believe that God has forgiven him, but actually live in a form of purgatory as he believes if he chastens himself emotionally and mentally for a certain number of days he will be able to get back on to the same spiritual plain. I have a minor neurosis about sleeping in the morning. I have a strong conviction that I must not sleep after 6.30. If I do happen to sleep in, I feel I must work harder the next night or do something a little harder to make up for that extra time. This is not a question of spirituality, but of temperament.

Other Christians live a whole day in frustration because they were unable to get their quiet-time first thing in the morning. They really believe that the devil is going to pounce on them extra hard. Actually the Bible does not even mention quiet-time. The devil is going to attack us anyway whether we miss our quiet-time or not. Let us aim for perfection, but not become a neurotic over it.

We must learn to handle our mistakes. In any situation with many people operating in different countries and languages there are bound to be mistakes. If we cannot absorb our own mistakes as well as those of others, we will crack up. One of our main problems in this area is that most of us are young and have not been involved in other Christian or secular work, but we have read Christian books and have a high ideal as to what a true disciple can and should be. I believe in reading Christian books and biographies of great men of God. However, they can lead on to an evangelical fairy land. These biographies often paint everything rosy. The difficulties and weak points of the Christian under discussion are left out. This is particularly true of books written some years ago.

The inner history of many missions and societies might shock you. Some of the great men of God might surprise you by their inconsistencies and mistakes. These are men God has used despite these things. We must realise perfection is our goal, for in Christ we are perfect. In 1 Corinthians we read about the most carnal Christians in the New Testament. Yet, Paul opens his letter by saying that he is writing to those who are sanctified. From reading further we realise that some of these people were living in sin and committing all kinds of terrible things, but the apostle Paul knew how to handle people's failures and how to discipline people, keeping the balance. This is perhaps what made him great. It is very important to have the balance in these matters.

Children or Men?

The sixth balance involves conquering spiritual immaturity. There is a lot of spiritual immaturity in the Christian world and in the church. This brother does it so I can; he is going there, I want to go there; or, he has got this so I want that. This is immaturity. The truly mature Christian can say, 'Others may, I cannot.' 'Others may, I won't.' For a number of years I believed God did not want me to have a wrist watch, but I never preached against wrist watches. Now I have a wrist watch, and it is most helpful, but for a long time I was able to be without one though many suggested I get one.

It is amazing how easily we get the 'I want' bug, just because we see someone else has it and not because we need it. Generally, if we really need a thing we can obtain it. But how often we are so immature that when we see somebody else with something then we suddenly realise we want it also. We even get to the absurd place whereby one person has a special snack served and we get jealous. Or we discover someone who we thought was a very dedicated disciple has a tape recorder which we don't have, and we decide we also should have one. This is 'keeping up with the Joneses'. God's way is revolutionary as demonstrated in the life of Paul. For him others could have it, but he could not; others needed it but he did not. Don't base your spiritual life on even the most dedicated Christian you know. Base it rather on the Word of God and what the Lord Jesus reveals to you. Perhaps the Lord has shown you things you should not do. Then you meet some mature Christian who is doing these things. This can be most upsetting unless you are maturing. Remember, some people have natural ability which may not be real dedication. A man may be living like a king, breaking all the principles you believe in concerning forsaking all and living the life of discipleship, and yet winning more souls in one week than you do in one year. Remember, this man might be even more used if he were living the sort of revolutionary life Jesus taught. He may be weak on some points that are far more familiar to you, but strong on some points you do not see.

Let us beware of getting worked up by the way people spend money. This is always a sensitive area. There are some men, particularly in the west, who will spend more money in one week for a hotel room and food than a hundred of us would spend in a month. Yet God is using them. How can this be? It can be because God is Sovereign, God is great, God is a God of Love, God is a God of Mercy and looks upon their hearts. Let us look to God and run our lives the way He shows us, being able to say, 'Others may, we cannot.' This is the sign of true spiritual maturity.

Realistic or Legalistic?

Finally, learn to distinguish the difference between what is biblical and what is personal conviction. It is possible to get a Bible verse for almost anything. You can defend almost anything from the Bible, but only if you are willing to take isolated Bible verses out of their context.

Certain things we do are not biblical principles. These are principles we have accepted as those which have the least amount of problems. There will always be problems, and we must learn to discern between strong, definite and unmovable principles and principles we need to operate in a particular setting. For example, there is nothing biblical about the time schedule for eating. It is just a matter of practicality.

The spiritually mature person can discern between what is biblical and what is unique in particular situations. There are some things that are unique to us which cannot be forced into another situation. No doubt there may be some men who after they have left us will shake their wives at 6.30 a.m. saying, 'But darling, you've got to get up for your exercises, or you are not a true disciple.' When she rolls over and says, 'Please I want to sleep,' the poor fellow won't know what to do. We need *spiritual balance*.

Other books by George Verwer

Hunger for Reality
A powerful plea for a new depth of commitment and reality in our own walk with God. A message that has changed the lives of many Christians today.

Literature Evangelism
A challenge to Christians to present the Gospel through the printed page, with practical advice as to the many ways in which this can be done.

A Revolution of Love and Balance
Four messages on different aspects of commitment and discipleship. It is an appeal to Christians to take seriously the revolutionary teachings of Jesus, and be balanced by the experience of His love.

Messages by George Verwer on STL Message Tapes

Three messages on 'Spiritual Growth'
1 Foundations for Spiritual Growth
2 Spiritual Balance
3 Hindrance to Spiritual Growth
Make Your Life Count (One album of six tapes)
A Breath from the Book of Acts
Day by Day Reality
Emotional and Mental Survival
Fiery Darts of Immorality
Great Men of Faith
The Life of Paul (Part 1)
The Life of Paul (Part 2)
A Life Worth Living
Misconceptions about Missions
Thoughts from the Book of Proverbs

All these books and tapes are available from your local Christian bookshop or direct from STL Mail Order, P.O. Box 48, Bromley, Kent, or Merrion Press, 10 D'Olier Street, Dublin 2, Eire.